Penguin Reference Books
Facts in Focus

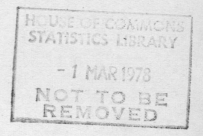

Facts in Focus

compiled by the
Central Statistical
Office

Fourth Edition

Penguin Books
in association with
H.M. Stationery Office

Penguin Books Ltd, Harmondsworth,
Middlesex, England
Penguin Books, 625 Madison Avenue,
New York, New York 10022, U.S.A.
Penguin Books Australia Ltd, Ringwood,
Victoria, Australia
Penguin Books Canada Ltd, 2801 John Street,
Markham, Ontario, Canada L3R 1B4
Penguin Books (N.Z.) Ltd,
182–190 Wairau Road,
Auckland 10, New Zealand

First published 1972
Second edition 1974
Third edition 1975
Fourth edition 1978

Made and printed in Great Britain by
Richard Clay (The Chaucer Press) Ltd,
Bungay, Suffolk
Set in Monotype Univers

Contents

Contents

Contents

Contents

Contents

Contents

Contents

Foreword

Statistics are part of our way of life. Politicians, professional and amateur, argue over them; businessmen and administrators plan with them; trade unionists bargain around them. They are essential to the academic researcher; and every social science student must know where to find a wide range of data. The main provider of statistics in this country is the Government Statistical Service and a vast array of detailed figures is regularly made available through a variety of specialist publications.

Facts in Focus adds a new dimension to the publication of statistics by offering, in inexpensive paperback form, a summarized collection of the most interesting and important of these figures. It carries government statistics from the reference library shelf into the home, the study and the office.

Briefly, our object has been to provide, in one compact volume, a selection of statistics on those topics thought to be of greatest current interest. If you can settle the facts of an argument more often than not by reference to this book then our choice will have been about right. And if you do need to look further, then the index to sources at the back will set you on the right track.

The fourth edition has broadly the same coverage as before but the information has, of course, been brought up to date. Wherever possible, figures are given for 1966, 1971 and 1975 or 1976 — whichever was available at the time of going to print — to show trends over a decade, while most of the charts extend over a longer period. Many of the 1976 figures are provisional and will be subject to some revision. For example, some of the national income and balance of payments figures are based on the preliminary estimates issued in March; final figures are published later in the year in the Central Statistical Office's 'Blue Book' and 'Pink Book'.

This sort of book cannot, in any case, give the very latest figures for monthly economic statistics like unemployment, prices and the trade figures. These are issued regularly by the Government Statistical Service and usually appear in the national press. For the really enthusiastic, they are brought together monthly in *Economic Trends* which also has a list of the release dates of all of these series in the following month.

Facts in Focus is arranged under nineteen chapter headings. Footnotes have been kept to the minimum but many are necessary to explain the nature of the figures in the tables. An important qualification included in every table is whether the figures cover the whole of the United Kingdom or only a part of it. Many economic series are prepared only on a United Kingdom basis; social statistics, on the other hand, are often produced separately for each country and, because of differences in legal and administrative systems, cannot always be combined into tables for the United

Kingdom. In any case, where it was thought more helpful to show separate
figures for each country this has been done. Whatever the reason,
care is needed to ensure that, when comparisons are made, the data
are consistent.

This pocketbook of statistics has been prepared by the Central Statistical
Office together with the Statistics Divisions of Government Departments.
Some of the statistics are provided by organizations outside the Government
Statistical Service, such as nationalized boards and trade associations,
whose help is gratefully acknowledged.

Substantial resources go into the compilation of official statistics and the
Government Statistical Service attaches great importance to their effective
dissemination. We very much welcome this opportunity to co-operate with
Penguin Books in producing a widely-distributed handbook of statistics and,
through this, to contribute to better decisions and more informed discussion
of public affairs.

Central Statistical Office
Great George Street
London SW1P 3AQ
July 1977

Symbols and conventions used

Units of measurement

Tables of conversion factors from and to metric equivalents are given on pages 246–7.

Rounding of figures

In tables where figures have been rounded to the nearest final digit there may be an apparent slight discrepancy between the sum of the constituent items and the total as shown.

Symbols

The following symbols have been used throughout:

.. = not available

— = nil or negligible (less than half the final digit shown)

· = not applicable

I Population and vital statistics

Table 1

Home population
United Kingdom

thousands

	United Kingdom	England and Wales	Scotland	Northern Ireland
Census Figures				
1901	38,237	32,528	4,472	1,237
1911	42,082	36,070	4,761	1,251
1921	44,027	37,887	4,882	1,258[1]
1931	46,038	39,952	4,843	1,243[1]
1951	50,225	43,758	5,096	1,371
1961	52,709	46,105	5,179	1,425
1971	55,515	48,750	5,229	1,536
Mid-year estimates[2]				
1965	54,218	47,540	5,210	1,468
1966	54,500	47,824	5,201	1,476
1967	54,800	48,113	5,198	1,489
1968	55,049	48,346	5,200	1,503
1969	55,263	48,540	5,208	1,514
1970	55,421	48,680	5,214	1,527
1971	55,610	48,854	5,217	1,538
1972	55,793	49,038	5,210	1,545
1973	55,933	49,175	5,212	1,547
1974	55,965	49,201	5,217	1,547
1975	55,943	49,199	5,206	1,537
1976[4]	55,928	49,184	5,205	1,538
Population projections[3]				
1981	55,697	48,977	5,188	1,532
1991	56,712	49,844	5,304	1,566
2001	57,535	50,557	5,378	1.600
2011	57,706	50.707	5,385	1,613

1. Estimated figures.
2. The estimates for 1965–74 are based on the final results of the 1971 census.
3. Mid-1976 based projections of total population.
4. Provisional.

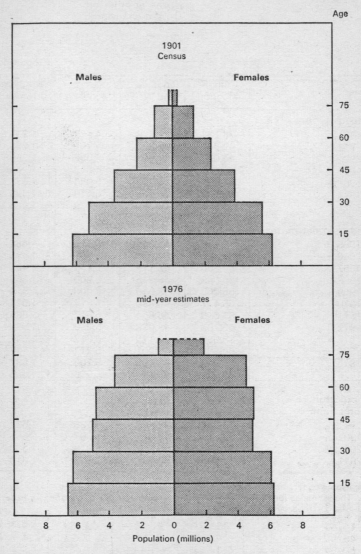

Chart 1: Population and age distribution of the United Kingdom

Table 2

**Sex and regional distribution
of the home population, 1976;[1]
Projection of the total population
by sex and age group
United Kingdom**

	Mid-year estimates		thousands
	Total	Males	Females
United Kingdom	55,928	27,219	28,709
Standard regions of England:			
North	3,122	1,533	1,589
Yorkshire and Humberside	4,892	2,384	2,508
East Midlands	3,733	1,842	1,891
East Anglia	1,803	894	909
South East	16,894	8,183	8,711
South West	4,254	2,056	2,198
West Midlands	5,165	2,552	2,614
North West	6,554	3,166	3,388
England	46,418	22,610	23,808
Wales	2,767	1,344	1,423
Scotland	5,205	2,504	2,702
Northern Ireland	1,538	762	776

	1976 based projections			thousands
Age group	1981	1991	2001	2011
Males				
0–4	1,646	2,289	2,000	1,967
5–14	4,169	3,592	4,444	3,801
15–44	12,055	12,611	12,083	11,966
45–59	4,693	4,627	5,278	5,803
60–64	1,371	1,336	1,293	1,630
65 and over	3,241	3,352	3,253	3,349
Females				
0–14	1,555	2,163	1,889	1,858
5–14	3,941	3,391	4,198	3,587
15–44	11,607	12,082	11,523	11,381
45–59	4,808	4,689	5,291	5,732
60–64	1,553	1,466	1,381	1,764
65 and over	5,053	5,154	4,902	4,868

1. Provisional.

Table 3

Estimates of the population of New Commonwealth and Pakistani ethnic origin[1] **Great Britain**

thousands

	Mid-year to mid-year		
	1973/74	1974/75	1975/76
Population at beginning of period	1,547	1,615	1 691
Births	+44	+44	+45
Deaths[2]	−5	−5	−5
Natural increase	+39	+39	+40
Migration	+29	+37	+40
Change in year	+68	+76	+80
Population at end of period	1,615	1,691	1,771
Percentage of home population at end of period	3·0	3·1	3·3

1. 1971 Census of Population was used as a starting point.
2. Including an estimate of deaths of children of New Commonwealth or Pakistani ethnic origin born in the United Kingdom.

Table 4

**Population of conurbations and
cities and towns with over
200,000 persons at mid-1971
United Kingdom**

Mid-year estimates[1] thousands

	1951	1961	1971	Percentage change 1971/1961
Conurbations				
Greater London	8,206	7,977	7,441	−6·7
West Midlands	2,257	2,370	2,371	−0·04
South East Lancashire	2,411	2,419	2,400	−0·8
Central Clydeside	1,760	1,804	1,723	−4·5
West Yorkshire	1,683	1,699	1,736	+2·2
Merseyside	1,382	1,380	1,264	−8·4
Tyneside	835	853	803	−5·9
Cities and towns[2]				
Birmingham	1,112	1,105	1,014	−8·2
Glasgow	1,093	1,056	894	−15·3
Liverpool	789	741	605	−18·4
Manchester	700	657	546	−16·9
Sheffield	540	537	518	−3·5
Leeds	504	508	502	−1·2
Edinburgh	475	474	453	−4·4
Bristol	444	436	426	−2·3
Teesside	334	374	395	+5·6
Belfast	444	416	360	−13·5
Coventry	266	316	334	+5·7
Nottingham	308	311	298	−4·2
Bradford	290	295	294	−0·3
Kingston-upon-Hull	299	302	285	−5·6
Leicester	285	286	282	−1·4
Cardiff	263	284	277	−2·5
Wolverhampton	243	261	269	+3·1
Stoke-on-Trent	278	276	265	−4·0
Plymouth	237	240	246	+2·5
Newcastle-upon-Tyne	291	268	221	−17·5
Derby	196	212	219	+3·3
Sunderland	206	218	216	−0·9
Southampton	190	205	213	+3·9
Portsmouth	246	225	205	−8·9

1. Population figures based on 1971 boundaries.
2. All the cities and towns are County Boroughs with the exception of Edinburgh and Glasgow which are County Councils.

Table 5

Composition of private[1] households in Great Britain

1966 and 1971 Censuses of Population

thousands

	Total number of house-holds	Number of households with:			
		No[2] families	1 family	2 families	3 or more families
1966 Census[3]					
Total number of households	16,937	3,287	13,334	312	5
Number of persons in household:					
1	2,572	2,572	—	—	—
2	5,158	588	4,570	—	—
3	3,592	95	3,498	—	—
4	3,042	22	2,932	88	—
5	1,480	7	1,375	98	—
6	656	2	580	73	1
7	238	—	208	28	1
8	107	—	93	12	1
9	49	—	42	6	1
10 or more	43	—	35	6	1
1971 Census[3]					
Total number of households	18,317	4,068	13,986	258	5
Number of persons in household:					
1	3,320	3,320	—	—	—
2	5,771	623	5,149	—	—
3	3,458	91	3,367	—	—
4	3,148	24	3,052	72	—
5	1,515	7	1,432	76	—
6	654	3	595	56	1
7	252	1	225	26	1
8	112	—	97	13	1
9	48	—	40	7	1
10 or more	40	—	30	8	2

1. A private household comprises one person living alone or a group of persons living together, partaking of meals prepared together and benefiting from a common housekeeping.

2. A family is a married couple, alone or with never-married children of any age, or a lone parent with never-married children.   3. 10 per cent sample.

Table 6

Births[1]
United Kingdom
Analysis by sex and legitimacy

	United Kingdom	England and Wales	Scotland	Northern Ireland
Live births (thousands)				
Male				
1966	504	437	49·8	17·3
1971	464	403	44·5	16·5
1976	347[2]	300[2]	33·5	13·5
Female				
1966	476	413	46·8	15·9
1971	438	380	42·3	15·3
1976	328[2]	284[2]	31·4	12·8
Total				
1966	980	850	96·5	33·2
1971	902	783	86·7	31·8
1976	676[2]	584[2]	64·9	26·4
Live births per 1,000 women aged 15–44				
1966	91·7	90·8	93·5	112·0
1971	84·8	84·0	85·6	108·6
1976	61·9[2]	60·8[2]	62·4	87·8
Illegitimate as percentage of all live births				
1966	7·6	7·9	6·4	3·1
1971	8·2	8·4	8·1	3·8
1976	9·0[2]	9·2[2]	9·3	5·0
Stillbirths per 1,000 total births				
1966	15	15	16	16
1971	13	12	13	14
1976	10[2]	10[2]	10	10

1. Figures for England and Wales are the number of births actually occurring in the year. Figures for Scotland and Northern Ireland are the number of live births registered in the year.
2. Provisional.

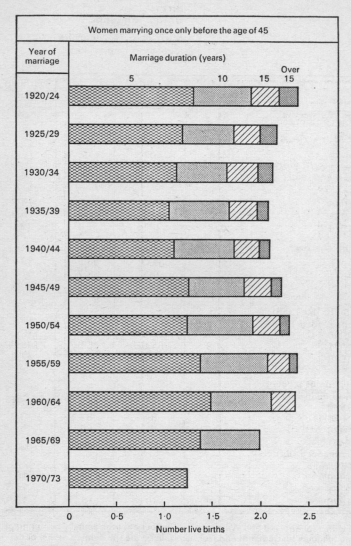

**Chart 2: Average family
size by duration of marriage
Great Britain**

Table 7

**Marriages
United Kingdom**

Analysis by sex, age and
previous marital status

thousands

	1966	1971	1975
Total marriages	437	459	431
Age at marriage			
Males			
Under 18 years	4	4	4
18 and under 21	68	73	64
21–24	186	197	152
25–29	91	91	100
30–34	30	30	37
35–44	27	27	34
45–54	14	16	20
55 and over	17	21	21
Females			
Under 18 years	26	30	23
18 and under 21	156	146	131
21–24	149	162	129
25–29	44	53	64
30–34	17	19	26
35–44	20	20	26
45–54	13	15	17
55 and over	11	14	14
Previous marital status			
Males	437	459	431
Single	388	394	340
Widowed	21	20	19
Divorced	28	45	71
Females	437	459	431
Single	392	398	342
Widowed	18	19	19
Divorced	27	42	69

Table 8

**Divorce
England and Wales**

Analysis by age at marriage and
duration of marriage at divorce

thousands

	1966	1971	1976
Total divorces	39·1	74·4	126·7
Age at marriage			
Males			
Under 20	3·7	8·2	15·9
20–24	21·1	40·8	69·3
25–29	9·0	16·1	25·4
30–39	4·0	6·9	11·4
40–49	0·9	1·6	3·1
50 and over	0·4	0·8	1·5
Females			
Under 20	14·0	27·8	48·8
20–24	18·0	34·0	56·5
25–29	4·1	7·5	12·1
30–39	2·1	3·6	6·4
40–49	0·6	1·1	2·0
50 and over	0·2	0·4	1·0
Duration of marriage at divorce (years)			
0–4	4·6	9·7	22·4
5–9	12·6	22·6	38·2
10–14	8·3	14·4	23·7
15–19	5·8	9·4	16·2
20 and over	7·7	18·4	26·0

Table 9

Adoptions
England and Wales

Age and legitimacy of children
adopted under registered orders

number

	1966	1971	1976
All ages			
Male	11,616	11,013	8,939
Female	11,176	10,482	8,682
Legitimate			
Male			
Under 6 months	106	52	30
6–11 "	236	125	56
12–23 "	187	78	72
2–4 years	592	704	728
5–9 "	805	1,531	2,100
10 years and over	524	800	1,401
Female			
Under 6 months	99	46	22
6–11 "	230	82	71
12–23 "	169	88	55
2–4 years	590	656	697
5–9 "	815	1,626	2,112
10 years and over	559	800	1,409
Illegitimate			
Male			
Under 6 months	2,319	1,746	783
6–11 "	3,666	2,123	1,037
12–23 "	867	735	350
2–4 years	1,214	1,862	1,015
5–9 "	656	945	982
10 years and over	444	312	385
Female			
Under 6 months	2,304	1,627	687
6–11 "	3,348	1,979	922
12–23 "	810	648	297
2–4 years	1,182	1,731	1,002
5–9 "	642	871	967
10 years and over	428	328	441

Table 10
Deaths
United Kingdom
Analysis by sex and age

thousands

	1966	1971	1975
Total deaths	643·8	645·1	662·5
Males	329·8	328·5	335·0
Under 1 year	11·1	9·4	6·4
1–4	1·9	1·4	1·1
5–14	1·8	1·9	1·7
15–44	16·8	15·2	14·7
45–64	92·6	87·9	83·2
65 and over	205·5	212·8	227·9
Females	314·0	316·5	327·5
Under 1 year	8·1	6·8	4·8
1–4	1·4	1·1	0·9
5–14	1·1	1·1	0·9
15–44	10·1	9·0	8·7
45–64	52·4	51·0	49·0
65 and over	240·8	247·5	263·2

rates per thousand home population

	1966	1971	1975
Males	12·5	12·2	12·3
Under 1 year[1]	22·0	20·2	17·8
1–4	0·9	0·8	0·7
5–14	0·4	0·4	0·4
15–44	1·6	1·4	1·3
45–64	14·3	13·6	13·2
65 and over	81·2	75·4	75·1
Females	11·2	11·1	11·4
Under 1 year[1]	17·1	15·5	14·2
1–4	0·8	0·6	0·5
5–14	0·3	0·3	0·2
15–44	0·9	0·8	0·8
45–64	7·5	7·4	7·3
65 and over	58·2	54·7	54·9

1. Rates per thousand live births.

Table 11

Migration into and out from the United Kingdom, by nationality and country of last permanent or intended future residence[1,2]

thousands

	1966[6]		1971		1976	
	In	Out	In	Out	In	Out
Total migrants	219·2	301·6	199·7	240·0	179·8	210·4
Commonwealth citizens	142·3	262·9	145·3	200·0	129·9	165·5
Country of last permanent or intended future residence:[1]						
Commonwealth countries						
Total	110·9	202·9	117·0	133·8	87·6	89·9
Australia	19·8	84·9	31·5	68·7	24·4	31·5
Canada	8·7	62·2	13·2	14·7	7·3	22·0
New Zealand	6·9	15·8	7·2	13·1	8·1	9·0
African countries	20·3	15·7	26·7	15·4	17·7	10·7
India, Pakistan[3], Bangladesh and Sri Lanka (Ceylon)	26·7	8·7	24·3	7·8	9·2	3·6
West Indies[4]	14·8	8·5	5·0	7·8	3·6	3·4
Other countries	13·6	7·0	9·1	6·2	17·4	9·8
Foreign countries						
Total	31·4	59·8	28·3	66·1	42·4	75·6
South Africa	4·7	12·3	5·1	19·5	7·9	19·6
United States	8·4	18·9	9·8	9·3	6·4	10·6
Other America	1·0	1·0	0·8	1·0	1·7	1·8
Western Europe[5]	13·0	18·7	8·9	26·5	17·4	22·7
Other countries	4·3	8·9	3·6	9·8	8·9	20·8
Aliens	76·9	38·7	54·4	40·1	49·8	44·9
Country of last permanent or future intended residence:[1]						
Commonwealth countries	1·7	4·5	1·1	3·5	0·9	1·2
Foreign countries						
Total	75·2	34·3	53·2	36·6	48·9	43·6
United States	14·3	8·1	12·4	7·3	10·0	10·3
EEC countries	27·8	13·0	14·0	14·4	9·8	13·6
Other Western Europe[5]	19·3	6·6	13·7	7·3	9·0	7·7
Other countries	13·8	6·6	13·1	7·5	20·1	12·0

1. For more than 12 months.
2. Excluding the Irish Republic throughout, and Denmark for 1966 and 1971.
3. Included with Foreign countries in 1976.
4. Including Guyana and Belize (formerly British Honduras).
5. Including Eastern Europe for 1976.
6. Revised figures.

Population changes

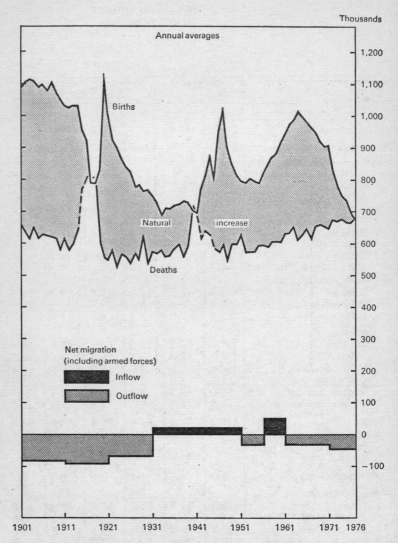

**Chart 3: Population changes
United Kingdom**

Table 12

**Life table 1973–75
United Kingdom**

Age	Males		Females	
	Number of survivors from 10,000 births	Expectation of life in years	Number of survivors from 10,000 births	Expectation of life in years
0	10,000	69·2	10,000	75·5
5	9,786	65·7	9,833	71·8
10	9,768	60·8	9,820	66·9
15	9,751	56·0	9,810	62·0
20	9,706	51·2	9,791	57·1
25	9,655	46·4	9,770	52·2
30	9,611	41·6	9,746	47·3
35	9,556	36·9	9,712	42·5
40	9,479	32·2	9,667	37·7
45	9,342	27·6	9,560	33·1
50	9,093	23·3	9,398	28·6
55	8,680	19·2	9,150	24·3
60	8,032	15·6	8,790	20·2
65	7,076	12·3	8,252	16·3
70	5,737	9·6	7,448	12·8
75	4,090	7·4	6,255	9·7
80	2,453	5·7	4,628	7·2
85	1,138	4·6	2,736	5·5

Table 13

**Government expenditure on the
national health service
United Kingdom**

	Years ended 31 March		£ million
	1966/67	1971/72	1976/77
Current expenditure			
Central government			
Hospital and community health services:[1]			
Hospital running expenses	758	1,341	4,183
Administration and other expenses	39	83	238
Family practitioner services:			
General medical services	112	196	382
Pharmaceutical services	163	249	616
General dental services	80	122	265
General ophthalmic services	23	28	80
Administration	9	14	—
less Payments by patients:			
Hospital services	−8	−13	−32
Pharmaceutical services	—	−25	−27
Dental services	−13	−26	−46
Ophthalmic services	−9	−14	−27
Total	−30	−78	−132
Departmental administration	12	23	62
Other services	13	28	123
Local health services expenditure[2]	127	146	—
Total current expenditure	1,306	2,152	5,817
Capital expenditure			
Central government	102	195	417
Local authorities[2]	12	15	—
Total capital expenditure	114	210	417
Total expenditure			
Central government	1,281	2,201	6,234
Local authorities[2]	139	161	—
Total government expenditure	1,420	2,362	6,234

1. Including school health service from 1 April 1974, previously included in education.
2. On 1 April 1974 local authority health services became the responsibility of central government, and from that date are included under the heading of community health services.

Table 14

Hospitals and family practitioner services
England and Wales

	1966		1971		1976	
	Thou-sands	Per thou-sand popu-lation	Thou-sands	Per thou-sand popu-lation	Thou-sands	Per thou-sand popu-lation
Hospitals						
Allocated beds	468	9·8	450	9·2	416	8·4
Occupied beds	393	8·2	368	7·5	828	6·7
Discharges and deaths	4,898	102·1	5,494	112·5	5,599	113·6
New out-patients during year	7,598	158·3	8,353	171·0	7,943	161·4
Total out-patients' attendances	31,359	653·5	34,820	712·7	34,029	693·8
New accident and emergency cases during year	7,145	148·9	8,329	170·5	9,232	188·8
Medical staff[1]	19·5	0·4	23·8	0·5	29·3	0·6
Nursing staff[1,2]	217·7	4·6	248·2	5·1	} 361·1[3]	0·7[3]
Midwifery staff[1,2]	13·8	0·3	14·6	0·3		
Professional and technical staff[1]	29·2	0·6	36·8	0·8	55·2[3]	1·1[3]
Family practitioner services						
General medical practitioners	21·3	0·47	21·9	0·45	23·4	0·48
General dental practitioners	10·4	0·22	11·0	0·23	12·1	0·25
Ophthalmic practitioners all types	7·1	0·15	6·6	0·14	7·2	0·15

1. Whole-time equivalent.
2. Excluding agency staff.
3. 1976 figures are provisional national health service numbers.

Table 15

Hospital facilities and use
England and Wales

	Unit	1966	1971	1976
In-patients (non-psychiatric)				
Average length of stay (estimated)	Days	16·2	14·0	12·9
Discharges and deaths per available bed per year	Number	18·2	20·5	21·6
Percentage of available beds occupied	Per cent	80·7	79·5	76·3
In-patients (psychiatric)				
Average length of stay (estimated)	Days	361·1	294·1	242·6
Discharges and deaths per available bed per year	Number	0·9	1·1	1·3
Percentage of available beds occupied	Per cent	91·1	88·3	88·4
Out-patients				
Total attendances per new out-patient	Number	4·1	4·2	4·3
Accident and Emergency				
Total attendances per new out-patient	Number	1·9	1·7	1·5
Total attendances for:				
Physiotherapy	Thousands	21,306	23,233	26,479
Occupational therapy	„	4,154	5,191	7,099
Radiotherapy treatment	„	1,093	1,120	1,204
Diagnostic X-ray (number of units of work)[1]	„	29,029	37,149	255,897

1. In 1972 radiological unit values were revised. Figures for 1971 and 1976 are not comparable.

Table 16

Deaths
United Kingdom[1]

Analysis by cause

thousands

	1966	1971	1976
Males			
Deaths from natural causes – total	313·4	313·8	327·6
Cancer of the lung	25·5	28·4	30·1
Other cancer	40·8	43·0	46·0
Cerebrovascular diseases	36·7	36·0	33·5
Coronary disease, angina	80·2	95·8	103·2
Respiratory diseases	49·8	46·4	54·4
Other natural causes	80·4	64·2	60·5
Deaths by violence – total	16·3	14·8	14·3
Transport accidents	6·6	6·0	5·3
Other accidents	6·4	5·9	5·6
Suicide	3·1	2·5	2·6
Homicide and war	0·2	0·3	0·7
Females			
Deaths from natural causes – total	302·3	305·0	328·1
Cancer of the lung	5·0	6·4	7·9
Other cancer	51·3	54·8	57·8
Cerebrovascular diseases	54·6	56·4	54·1
Coronary disease, angina	52·4	69·5	78·9
Respiratory diseases	35·7	35·4	50·2
Pregnancy, childbirth, abortion	0·3	0·2	0·1
Other natural causes	103·0	82·4	79·2
Deaths by violence – total	11·7	11·6	10·8
Transport accidents	2·5	2·7	2·3
Other accidents	6·7	6·8	6·3
Suicide	2·4	1·9	1·7
Homicide and war	0·2	0·2	0·4

1. Figures for 1971 and 1976 are based on the eighth revision of the International Classification of Diseases. The 1966 figures were based on the seventh revision. Thus figures for 1971 and 1976 are not strictly comparable with those for 1966.

Table 17

Preventive medicine
England and Wales

thousands

	1966	1971	1976
Mass miniature radiography			
Total number of examinations	3,261	1,972	1,280[1]
Male	1,888	1,070	672[1]
Female	1,373	902	608[1]
Persons with tuberculosis requiring treatment or close supervision – rate per 1,000 examinations – total	1·0	0·9	1·1[1]
Male	1·2	1·2	1·4[1]
Female	0·7	0·7	0·7[1]
Examinations for cervical cancer			
Positive cases detected per 1,000 cases examined	..	4·4	4·8
Vaccination and immunization			
Number aged under 16 who completed a primary course against:			
Diphtheria	772·2	715·2	509·8
Whooping cough	693·8	642·5	247·6
Poliomyelitis	866·8	711·7	519·1
Tetanus	836·5	750·9	532·5
Numbers vaccinated against tuberculosis (all ages)	479·0	580·5	649·0

1. 1974 figure.

Table 18

Notifications of certain infectious diseases United Kingdom

number

	1966	1971	1975
Diphtheria	20	17	12
Typhoid and paratyphoid fevers	286	245	301
Food poisoning	5,538	8,304	10,301
Scarlet fever	23,183	13,878	10,235
Whooping cough	21,814	19,365	9,923
Smallpox	62	—	—
Dysentery	26,287	15,232	9,375
Measles	355,016	155,188	158,572
Acute poliomyelitis	26	8	4
Ophthalmia neonatorum	652	470	330[1]
Tuberculosis – respiratory	14,717	10,799	9,579
Tuberculosis – non-respiratory	2,791	2,958	2,9ɔ5

1. Great Britain only.

Table 19

New cases treated at sexually transmitted disease clinics England and Wales

number

		1966	1971	1976
Total cases of S.T.D.	male	112,926	192,953	236,178
	female	51,837	114,711	153,846
Syphilis	male	2,454	2,284	3,110
	female	1,224	855	927
Gonorrhoea	male	27,921	39,055	38,115
	female	9,562	18,516	22,011
Other	male	22,595	44,889	61,589
	female	25,102	56,595	75,953
Total non-S.T.D. cases seen but not requiring treatment at the clinic	male	29,414	45,967	56,931
	female	15,946	25,167	34,458

Table 20

Abortions[1]
Great Britain
Analysis by age, marital status and
place of abortion

number

	1973	1974	1975
Total	119,134	118,016	114,578
Place of abortion			
NHS hospitals	62,883	63,516[2]	58,103[2]
Private hospitals and clinics	56,251	54,512[2]	56,486[2]
Marital status			
Single women	56,123[3]	57,321	56,376
Widowed, divorced and separated	11,673[3]	11,904	11,748
Married	50,123[3]	48,675	46,346
Not stated	147[3]	116	108
Age distribution			
Under 16 years	3,326	3,551	3,791
16–19	25,384	26,222	26,206
20–34	68,903	67,760	64,945
35 and over	19,656	18,810	17,755
Not stated	1,865	1,673	1,881
Women domiciled abroad as a percentage of all women obtaining abortions[4]	31·8	30·8	22·1

1. Resident women only.
2. Scottish women having abortions in England and Wales are notification figures.
3. Figures for Scottish residents having abortions in England and Wales, by marital status, are not available.
4. Including Northern Ireland.

Table 21

**National health service
family planning services
Great Britain**

thousands

	1974[1]	1975	1976
Clinic services (community and hospital)			
New patients	1,142·3	1,626·9	1,669·2
Attendances	2,743·9	4,116·0	4,090·1
Domiciliary services			
New patients	14·1	22·0	20·6
Visits by family planning staff	54·3	77·4	82·1

1. 1974 figures are for period 1 April to 31 December.

Table 22

**Registered handicapped persons
England**

thousands

	1966[1]	1972[1]	1976[1]
Blind			
Total – all ages	93·7	96·4	101·1
Under 16	2·1	2·0	2·2
16–64	26·7	25·6	24·8
65 and over	64·9	68·8	74·0
Partially sighted			
Total – all ages	28·7	35·7	42·9
Under 16	2·3	2·7	2·8
16–64	8·9	10·4	11·8
65 and over	17·5	22·6	28·4
Deaf			
Total – all ages	22·5	23·1	27·5
Under 16	2·7	2·7	3·4
16–64	15·7	15·7	17·2
65 and over	4·1	4·7	6·9
Hard of hearing			
Total – all ages	15·1	15·8	25·6
Under 16	1·6	1·2	1·2
16–64	5·3	4·7	5·8
65 and over	8·2	9·9	18·6
Others			
Total – all ages	150·0	304·2	657·2[2]
Under 16	3·8	8·9	15·9[2]
16–64	85·4	136·6	240·6[2]
65 and over	60·8	158·7	400·8[2]

1. Figures relate to 31 December prior to 1972 and to 31 March thereafter.
2. Increases due in part to a review of local authority lists of registered handicapped persons as a result of the Chronically Sick and Disabled Persons Act, 1970.

Table 23

Children in the care of local authorities
England and Wales
At 31 March   thousands

	1966	1971[1]	1975
All children in care	69·2	87·4	99·1
By age groups:			
Under two years	5·8	4·4	4·0
Two years but not of compulsory school age	9·5	9·0	8·3
Compulsory school age[2]	39·2	49·9	66·9
Over compulsory school age[2]	14·6	24·0	19·9
Admissions to care of local authority during year	54·5	71·0	62·2
Manner of accommodation:			
Boarded out	31·8	30·2	31·9
In lodgings or residential employment	1·8	1·9	2·0
In community homes provided, controlled or assisted by local authorities:[3]			
with observation and assessment facilities[4]	..	..	5·4
with education on the premises[4]	..	..	6·2
residential nurseries providing accommodation for children under the age of seven	3·0	2·5	2·0
other homes	7·9	7·4	20·1
Voluntary homes	4·9	5·5	4·3
Accommodation for handicapped children	2·1	2·3	2·7
Hostels	1·0	1·3	0·7
Under charge of parent, guardian, relative or friend	4·4	12·3	18·0
Other accommodation	3·1	3·3	4·8

1. The increase subsequent to 1966 results in part from the provision of the Children and Young Persons Act, 1969, that children aged under 19 subject on 1 January, 1971, to supervision following release from approved schools should from that date be deemed to be in the care of the local authority.

2. Due to changes in the school leaving age, figures for successive years are not strictly comparable.

3. Figures prior to 1975 are not strictly comparable as on 1 April, 1973, the community homes system, established in accordance with the provisions of the Children and Young Persons Act, 1969, came into operation. This system integrated the previously separate systems of approved schools, remand homes, children's homes and hostels.

4. Former remand homes and approved schools. On 1 January, 1971, the power of the Courts to commit to an approved school or to the care of a fit person was abolished and replaced by the power to commit to the care of a local authority. Children and young persons aged under 19, then subject to approved school orders or to supervision after release from an approved school, were then deemed to be subject to care orders. The number of children and young persons in remand homes and approved schools in 1966 was 9·6 thousands.

Table 24
**Drug addicts known to the
Home Office
United Kingdom**

At 31 December

	1974	1975	1976
Number known to be taking drugs	1,971	1,953	1,881
Males	1,459	1,438	1,389
Females	512	515	492
Age distribution			
Under 20 years	64	39	18
20–24	692	562	411
25–29	684	754	810
30–34	163	219	247
35–49	163	169	189
50 and over	197	193	188
Age not stated	8	17	18
Type of drug[1]			
Methadone	1,551	1,542	1,477
Heroin	392	316	253
Morphine	82	70	48
Cocaine	47	23	17
Pethidine	61	62	58
Dextromoramide	64	70	77
Dipipanone	76	133	159
Other drugs	11	7	7

1. Addicts who are receiving more than one drug are shown against each drug
they receive.

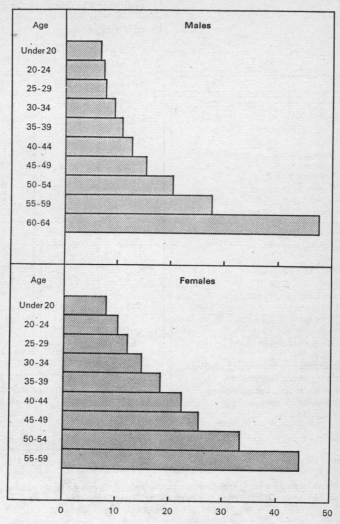

Chart 4: Days of certified sickness incapacity per person at risk, by age Great Britain 1973–74

Table 25

**Government expenditure on
social security benefits
United Kingdom**

£ million

	1966/67	1971/72	1976/77
General government current expenditure			
National insurance:			
Retirement pensions	1,300	2,091	5,573
Widows' benefits and guardians' allowances	146	203	439
Sickness benefits	272	434	1,091
Maternity benefits	38	44	72
Death grants	8	14	15
Unemployment benefits	85	250	578
Industrial injuries benefits	95	117	250
War pensions	118	136	290
Family allowances	156	359	564
Supplementary benefits:[1]			
Old persons	171	286	489
Unemployed persons	32	155	601
Sick persons	54	84	134
Other persons in need	52	140	384
Other non-contributory benefits:			
Old persons' pensions	—	24	38
Family income supplement	—	5	20
Attendance and mobility allowances[2]	—	6	144
Administration	120	230	845
Total government expenditure	2,647	4,578	11,527

1. National Assistance (including non-contributory old-age pensions) ceased
after 26 November 1966, when it was replaced by supplementary benefits.
2. Including mobility allowance from 1976 (1976/77 = £8 million).

Table 26

**Weekly rates of benefits
United Kingdom**

£ per week

	1966[1]	1971[1]	1976[2]
Family allowances:			
second child	0·40	0·90	1·50
third and each subsequent child	0·50	1·00	1·50
Retirement pension:			
single person	4·00	6·00	15·30
married couple	6·50	9·70	24·50
Unemployment benefit:			
men, single women and widows	4·00	6·00	12·90
married women	2·75	4·20	9·20
boys and girls under 18 years	2·275	3·30	9·20
Sickness benefit:			
men, single women and widows	4·00	4·00	12·90
married women	2·75	4·20	9·20
boys and girls under 18 years	2·275	3·30	9·20
Industrial injury benefit	6·75	8·75	15·65
Disablement pension	6·75	10·00	25·00
Maternity benefit:			
allowance for insured women	4·00	6·00	12·90
Widows' benefit:			
Widows' pension	4·00	6·00	15·30
Widowed mothers' allowance:	4·00	6·00	15·30
addition for first child	2·00	2·95	7·45
addition for second child	1·60	2·05	5·95
each additional child	1·50	1·95	5·95
Attendance allowance	—	4·80	12·20[3]
Increase for dependants (short-term benefits):			
one adult	2·50	3·70	8·00
first child	1·125	1·85	4·05
second child	0·725	0·95	2·55
each additional child	0·725	0·85	2·55

1. At 1 January.
2. At September except for Attendance Allowance which is December.
3. A reduced rate of £8·15 is payable for attendance by day or night.

Table 27

**Supplementary benefits:
weekly scale rates[1]
Great Britain**

£ per week

	1967 October	1971 September	1976 November	
	Basic rate	Basic rate	Basic rate	Long-term[2] rate
Single householder	4·30	5·80	12·70	15·70
Married couple[3]	7·05	9·45	20·65	24·85
Any other person:				
aged 21 years and over	3·55	4·60	10·15	12·60
18–20	2·90	4·05	10·15	12·60
16–17	2·50	3·60	7·80	
13–15	1·85	3·00	6·50	
11–12	1·85	2·45	5·35	
5–10	1·50	2·00	4·35	
under 5	1·25	1·70	3·60	
Long-term addition	0·45	0·50	—	
Long-term addition for age 80 years and over	—	0·25	0·25	

1. Scale rates for requirement other than rent, which is allowed for in addition.
2. From 1 October 1973 the long-term addition has been incorporated in the long-term rate.
3. Including couples cohabiting as man and wife.

Table 28

**Supplementary benefits: number[1] of persons receiving weekly payment and average amounts of payments
Great Britain**

	1967		1971		1976[2]	
	Persons (thousands)	Average amount (£)	Persons (thousands)	Average amount (£)	Persons (thousands)	Average amount (£)
All supplementary benefits	2,559	2·76	2,909	3·94	2,940	··
All supplementary pensions	1,806	1·95	1,919	2·52	1,687	6·61
Retirement pensioners and national insurance widows over 60	1,619	1·60	1,816	2·27	1,592	5·92
Others over pension age	187	4·99	103	6·93	95	18·17
All supplementary allowances	753	4·66	990	6·70	1,253	··
Unemployed with national insurance benefit	86	2·31	129	2·99	} 654	··
Unemployed without national insurance benefit	138	7·11	258	9·09		
Sick and disabled with national insurance benefit	164	2·05	146	2·36	74	7·08
Sick and disabled without national insurance benefit	146	4·94	159	6·60	169	13·92
National insurance widows under 60	60	1·94	65	2·60	28	7·29
Women with dependent children	142	7·46	213	10·23	303	24·72
Miscellaneous	17	5·15	20	7·85	25	20·25

1. On a selected day in November/December each year.
2. Because of industial action in some unemployment benefit offices, 1976 figures for unemployed cases and totals (i.e. supplementary allowances and supplementary benefits) are estimated and the average payment figures are missing.

Table 29

National insurance: number of persons receiving benefit Great Britain

At 31 December   thousands

	1966	1971	1976
Unemployment benefit	276	459	587[1]
Retirement pensions – total	6,540	7,647	8,417
Males	2,192	2,611	2,962
Females	4,348	5,035	5,455
Widows' benefits	580	564	486
Guardians' allowances, orphans' pensions and individual children's allowances	5	5	5
Industrial disablement pensions	202	205	201[2]

1. Figure for May 1976.
2. At 1 September 1975.

Table 30

Family allowances Great Britain

31 December   thousands

	1966	1971	1976
Families receiving allowances			
All families	3,944	4,323	4,445
Families with:			
2 children	2,336	2,589	2,891
3 children	991	1,110	1,082
4 children	382	413	340
5 or more children	235	212	132
Total number of children (including first child in families receiving allowances)	10,500	11,327	11,105
Families with one child (estimated)	3,000	2,648	2,767

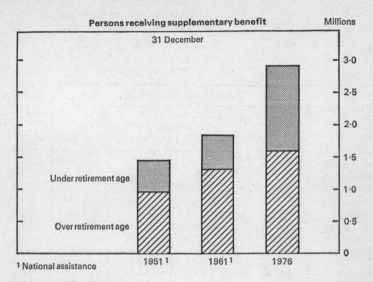

Persons receiving supplementary benefit · Millions

31 December

Under retirement age

Over retirement age

1 National assistance

1951 ¹   1961 ¹   1976

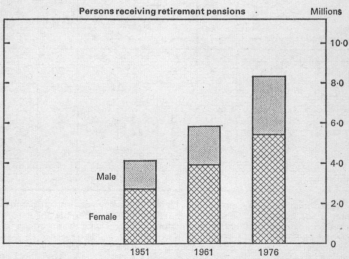

Persons receiving retirement pensions · Millions

Male

Female

1951   1961   1976

Chart 5: Persons receiving:
Supplementary benefit:
Retirement pensions
Great Britain

Table 31

Family income supplement: families by size and weekly rate[1] Great Britain

29 March 1977[2]   thousands

	Weekly rate in range					All famil- ies	Average weekly rate (£)
	£0·20 to £1·90	£2·00 to £3·90	£4·00 to £5·90	£6·00 to £7·90	£8·00 and over		
Families receiving supplements							
All two-parent families[3]	11	13	9	6	7	46	4·31
Number of children in family:							
1	2	2	2	1	1	9	4·13
2	4	4	2	2	2	13	4·09
3	3	3	2	1	1	11	4·05
4	2	2	1	1	1	7	4·60
5	1	1	1	1	1	4	4·92
6 or more	—	—	—	—	1	2	5·91
All one-parent families[3]	7	9	8	6	6	36	4·74
Number of children in family:							
1	4	5	5	3	3	20	4·54
2	2	2	2	2	2	10	4·69
3	1	1	1	1	1	4	5·14
4	—	—	—	—	—	2	5·99
5	—	—	—	—	—	—	6·24
6 or more	—	—	—	—	—	—	7·35

1. The maximum weekly supplement is £8·50 for a family with one child and an addition of 50p for each additional child in families with two or more children. There are approximately 4,000 families with one child receiving the maximum payment of £8·50, and 6,000 families with two or more children receiving maximum payments according to the number of children in the family. From 19 July 1977, the prescribed amount for one child is £41·50, increasing by £3·50 for each additional child. The maximum weekly rates remain unchanged.

2. Provisional.

3. Number of children in two-parent families is 128,000 and in one-parent families is 61,000.

IV Justice and Law

Table 32

Police force
Authorized establishment and strength
United Kingdom

At December   number

	1966	1971	1976
Regular police, England and Wales[1]			
Authorized establishment	104,565	109,095	116,880
Strength			
Men	82,457	91,810	101,042
Women	3,199	3,831	6,997
Auxiliaries, England and Wales			
Special constables			
Men	40,241	28,080	19,046
Women	1,632	1,912	2,370
Cadets			
Youths	3,730	3,761	2,728
Girls	375	737	977
Traffic Wardens			
Men	1,867	3,266	2,925
Women	790	2,574	2,942
Civilians[2]	18,196	28,060	34,551
Regular police, Scotland[3]			
Authorized establishment			
Men	10,646	10,950	} 13,163[4]
Women	414	453	
Strength			
Men	9,729	10,399	11,577
Women	367	412	740
Royal Ulster Constabulary, Northern Ireland			
Strength			
Men	2,934	3,961	4,811
Women	57	142	442
Royal Ulster Constabulary Reserve, Northern Ireland			
Strength			
Men – part-time	—	1,284	3,148
full-time	—	—	816
Women – part-time	—	—	679
full-time	—	—	54

1. Excluding reserves.
2. Figures for 1971 and 1976 include part-time civilian employees on a two-to-one basis. Figures for 1966 do not include part-timers.
3. Including additional regular police.
4. Now shown as one figure (establishment only).

Table 33

Offences known to the police, persons proceeded against and persons found guilty

thousands

	1966	1971	1976
England and Wales			
Offences recorded as known to the police	1,316	1,666	2,136
Indictable offences			
Persons proceeded against	250	351	457
Persons found guilty	208	282	359
Non-indictable offences			
Persons proceeded against	1,269	1,445	1,753
Persons found guilty	1,213	1,366	1,657
Scotland			
Crimes			
Persons proceeded against	15·0	20·3	40·6
Charge proved without conviction or finding of guilt	2·6	2·2	1·9
Persons convicted or found guilty	11·2	16·3	34·6
Miscellaneous offences			
Persons proceeded against	70·2	103·0	183·6
Charge proved without conviction or finding of guilt	1·3	1·5	2·2
Persons convicted or found guilty	64·1	95·9	168·7
Northern Ireland			
Indictable offences			
Persons proceeded against	4·2	4·7	5·4
Persons found guilty	4·0	4·3	5·0
Non-indictable offences			
Persons proceeded against	38·9	39·2	41·5
Persons found guilty	36·3	35·4	38·7

Table 34

**Persons found guilty
England and Wales**

Analysis by type of offence and
sex of offender

thousands

	1974	1975	1976
All offences			
Indictable offences – total	375	402	415
Violence against the person			
Murder, manslaughter			
or infanticide	0·4	0·4	0·4
Wounding or assault	32	35	37
Other offences of violence	0·7	0·7	0·6
Sexual offences	7	7	7
Burglary	64	69	68
Robbery	3	3	4
Theft and handling stolen goods	204	219	226
Fraud and forgery	18	20	21
Criminal damage	36	38	41
Other indictable offences	10	10	11
Non-indictable offences – total	1,559	1,586	1,636
Motoring offences	1,173	1,181	1,211
Drunkenness	98	100	103
Assault	12	12	12
Wireless and Telegraphy Acts	34	33	35
Motor vehicle licences	85	94	102
Other offences	157	167	173
Sex of offender:			
Indictable offences			
Men	322	342	350
Women	53	60	65
Non-indictable offences			
Men	1,437	1,457	1,496
Women	122	129	141

Table 35

Persons found guilty of indictable offences or crimes England and Wales

Analysis by age and sex of offender

Numbers per 100,000 population

	1972	1973	1974	1975	1976
Males					
Under 14	1,229	1,246	1,406	1,291	1,207
14–16	4,597	4,738	5,418	5,229	5,141
17–20	5,475	5,522	5,952	6,428	6,334
21–29	2,427	2,349	2,509	2,714	2,772
30 and over	567	543	587	642	687
All ages	1,484	1,464	1,603	1,694	1,726
Females					
Under 14	124	129	152	151	153
14–16	490	505	626	656	664
17–20	639	659	745	831	838
21–29	368	356	400	462	500
30 and over	137	126	151	172	192
All ages	219	210	247	278	299

Percentages and numbers by offence 1976

	Age groups					
	Under 14	14–16	17–20	21–29	30 and over	All ages
Males						
Murder, manslaughter or infanticide	—	—	0·1	0·1	0·1	0·1
Other offences of violence	2·8	6·4	10·6	12·6	10·7	10·0
Sexual offences	0·4	1·0	1·0	1·7	3·7	1·8
Burglary	37·3	32·3	18·7	15·1	8·2	18·6
Robbery	1·0	1·1	1·1	1·1	0·4	1·0
Theft and handling stolen goods	43·8	47·4	50·3	48·0	55·5	50·2
Fraud and forgery	0·7	1·0	3·2	6·7	8·0	4·8
Criminal damage	13·6	10·2	13·1	10·5	8·6	10·8
Total number of indictable offences (= 100%)	20,095	60,731	91,616	90,191	87,631	350,264
Females						
Murder, manslaughter or infanticide	—	—	—	0·1	0·1	0·1
Other offences of violence	4·7	9·6	5·1	4·9	2·7	4·5
Sexual offences	0·1	—	—	0·1	0·1	0·1
Burglary	16·0	10·7	5·6	2·5	0·9	3·8
Robbery	0·8	1·1	0·4	0·2	0·1	0·3
Theft and handling stolen goods	70·7	69·9	72·7	72·0	83·8	76·9
Fraud and forgery	1·7	2·8	9·5	10·3	5·3	6·9
Criminal damage	5·5	5·4	4·9	4·6	3·3	4·2
Total number of indictable offences (= 100%)	2,415	7,426	11,630	15,827	27,909	65,207

Table 36

**Driving, etc. after consuming alcohol or taking drugs[1]
England and Wales**

number

	1974	1975	1976
Total offences and alleged offences	66,821	70,456	63,288
Dealt with by written warning	47	62	95
Magistrates' Courts			
Dealt with by prosecution	66,774	70,394	63,193
Committed for trial	3,374	3,333	2,942
Charges withdrawn or dismissed	2,963	3,356	3,907
Findings of guilt	59,267	62,463	55,282
Other (not accounted for above)	1,170	1,242	1,062
Driving licences:			
Disqualifications	52,633	54,810	47,127
Endorsement without disqualification	1,924	2,342	2,090
Crown Court			
Offences for trial	3,997	3,717	3,128
Not tried	115	136	122
Acquitted	965	844	670
Findings of guilt	2,917	2,737	2,336
Driving licences:[2]			
Disqualifications	2,943	2,818	2,409
Endorsement without disqualification	237	248	219

1. Offences of driving, attempting to drive or being in charge of a motor vehicle while unfit, through drink or drugs, or with more than 80 mg of alcohol in 100 ml of blood, or of failing to provide a specimen.
2. Includes offences dealt with summarily and committed to the Crown Court for sentencing.

Table 37

Offences involving controlled drugs: persons found guilty United Kingdom

number

	1974	1975	1976
All offenders[1]	12,137	11,603	12,482
Persons found guilty of offences involving:			
Cocaine	394	402	336
Heroin	463	418	470
Methadone	482	513	425
Lysergamide (LSD)	827	791	624
Cannabis (all forms)	9,237	8,837	9,749
Amphetamines	1,503	1,525	1,903

1. Some offenders will have been found guilty of one or more offences in respect of different drugs.

Table 38

Legal aid in criminal proceedings England and Wales

number

	1971		1976	
	Ordered	Refused	Ordered	Refused
By Magistrates' Courts				
For proceedings before Magistrates' Courts	125,109	17,227	269,883	32,538
For appeals to the Crown Court	3,561	510	4,308	384
For persons committed to the Crown Court	46,783	346	73,603	393
By the Crown Court				
For proceedings before the Crown Court	9,042	148	9,263	209
For appeals to the Crown Court	1,543	192	4,010	91
By Court of Appeal Criminal Division	881	..	1,152	2

Table 39

**Legal aid in civil cases
Great Britain**

number

	1966/67	1970/71	1974/75
Number of legal aid certificates issued			
England and Wales			
Courts of first instance:			
High Courts of Justice[1]	54,691	82,450	123,130
County Courts	4,915	5,164	8,093
Magistrates' Courts[2]	49,362	69,890	68,234
Total cases	108,968	157,504	199,457
Out of court claims[3]	1,810	617	—
Courts of Appeal:			
House of Lords	14	15	15
Court of Appeal	224	257	296
Other	644	749	564
Total cases	882	1,021	875
Scotland			
All courts:			
House of Lords	4	3	2
Courts of Session	5,193	6,050	8,436
Sheriff Courts	2,706	2,768	3,092

1. Cases which may be brought in the High Court, including matrimonial cases brought in the County Court.
2. Legal aid came into Magistrates' Courts on 8 May 1961 and into the County Courts on 1 January 1956.
3. Bringing and defending claims without court procedure. Such claims have not beeen allowed since 1972/73.

Table 40

**Offences currently recorded[1]
as homicide
England and Wales**

number

	1974	1975	1976
Decided by court to be:			
Murder	154	96	91
Manslaughter	273	260	242
Infanticide	16	6	6
Court decision pending	1	2	43
No suspect	32	38	42
Suspect died, committed suicide or			
found insane	38	32	60
No further proceedings	13	11	9
Total offences	527	445	493
Number per million of population	10·7	9·0	10·0

1. Offence classifications as at June 1977.

Table 41

**Receptions into and populations
of prisons, borstals and
detention centres
England and Wales**

number

	1966	1971	1976
Receptions			
Untried	29,313	47,731	46,561
Convicted and awaiting sentence			
or inquiry[1]	24,459	27,663	22,882
Sentenced	50,205	60,427	68,479
Non-criminal prisoners	7,618	5,851	4,863
Alien prisoners[2]	110	745	1,037
Average population: all types of prisoner			
Sex:			
Male	32,127	38,673	40,161
Female	959	1,035	1,282
Type of prisoner:			
Untried	1,600	2,749	3,303
Convicted and awaiting sentence			
or inquiry	1,458	1,847	1,787
Total unsentenced	3,058	4,596	5,090
Sentenced			
Borstal training	5,560	6,071	6,206
Detention centre	1,627	1,730	1,756
Imprisonment	22,316	26,775	27,876
Other sentences[3]	24	—	—
Non-criminal	495	454	394
Alien	6	82	121
Total	33,086	39,708	41,443

1. Includes persons remanded under section 26 of the Magistrates' Court Act,
who were previously included under 'untried prisoners'. Figures for 1966 have
been adjusted to the 1971 and 1976 basis.
2. 1966 figures include those detained under the Commonwealth Immigrants
Act, 1962. Figures for 1971 and 1976 include persons detained under the
Immigration Act, 1971.
3. Included juveniles awaiting removal to approved schools in 1966. From
January 1971 Care orders replaced Approved School orders.

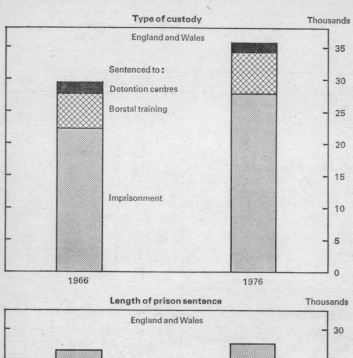

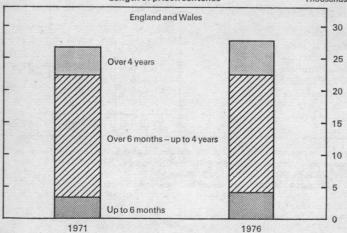

Chart 6: Population of prisons, borstals and detention centres

Table 42

Average daily prison population of sentenced prisoners England and Wales

Analysis by length of sentence and type of prison

number

	1966	1971	1976
Total serving prison sentences	21,746	26,775	27,876
Length of sentence			
Up to 6 months	..	3,365	4,063
Over 6 months, up to 18 months	..	8,669	8,255
Over 18 months, up to 4 years	..	10,356	10,227
Over 4 years, up to 10 years	..	3,300	3,713
Over 10 years[1]	..	1,085	1,618
Type of prison			
Local prisons	12,071	13,431	13,477
Other closed prisons	5,865	9,453	10,970
Open prisons	3,810	3,891	3,422
Young prisoners (as percentage of all inmates serving prison sentences)	4·3	5·2	7·8

1. Includes prisoners sentenced for life or detained at Her Majesty's Pleasure.

Table 43

Prisoners with previous institutional sentences England and Wales

number of receptions[1]

	1966	1971	1976
Number of previous institutional sentences – total	37,243	33,254	34,528
none	10,858	8,410	8,157
1–2	10,334	9,404	8,699
3–5	8,167	7,169	7,056
6–10	4,761	3,640	3,867
11 and over	2,261	1,768	2,022
Previous history not available	862	2,863	4,727

1. This table counts receptions of persons under sentence of imprisonment without the option of a fine.

Table 44

**Parliamentary elections
United Kingdom**

millions

	31 March 1966	18 June 1970	28 February 1974	10 October 1974
Number of electors[1]	35·96	39·62	39·80	40·26
Number of votes recorded[2]	27·26	28·34	31·33	29·19
as percentage of electorate	*75·8*	*71·5*	*78·7*	*72·5*
Analysis of votes cast:				
Communist	0·06	0·04	0·03	0·02
Conservative	11·42	13·14	11·96	10·46
Labour	13·06	12·18	11·65	11·46
Liberal	2·33	2·12	6·06	5·35
Other	0·39	0·86	1·62	1·90
as percentage of votes cast				
Communist	—	—	0·1	0·1
Conservative	42	46	38·2	35·8
Labour	48	43	37·2	39·2
Liberal	9	8	19·3	18·3
Other	1	3	5·2	6·6
Number of Members of Parliament elected				
Communist	0	0	0	0
Conservative	253	330	296	276
Labour	363	287	301	319
Liberal	12	6	14	13
Other	2	7	24	27
as percentage of Members of Parliament elected				
Communist	0	0	0	0
Conservative	40	52	46·6	43·5
Labour	58	46	47·4	50·2
Liberal	2	1	2·2	2·0
Other	—	1	3·8	4·2

1. The Representation of the Peoples Act lowered the minimum voting age from 21 to 18 years with effect from 16 February 1970.
2. Number of votes recorded relates only to voting for contested seats.

Table 45

**Stock of dwellings[1] : change,
tenure and region
United Kingdom**

thousands

	1967–71	1972–76
Stock of dwellings at end of period	19,457	20,607
Average annual net gain (+) or loss (−)	+269	+230
By nature of change:		
New construction – public sector	+192	+143
– private sector	+197	+169
Other gains	+6	+11
Slum clearance	−95	−72
Other losses	−31	−21
By tenure:		
Owner occupied	+258	+229
Rented from local authority or new town corporation	+159	+116
Rented from private owner including other tenures	−148	−115

1976   percentages

		Rented from	
	Owner occupied	Local authority or new town corporation	Private owner including other tenures
United Kingdom	53	32	15
England	55	29	16
North	45	40	15
Yorkshire and Humberside	53	33	14
East Midlands	56	29	15
East Anglia	56	27	17
South East	55	27	18
South West	62	22	16
West Midlands	55	34	11
North West	58	30	12
Wales	58	29	13
Scotland	34	54	12
Northern Ireland	48	38	14

1. Estimates by the Department of the Environment.

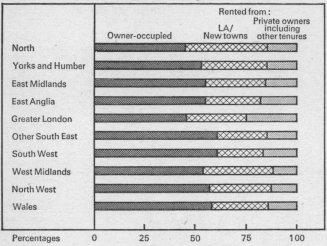

Tenure of dwellings

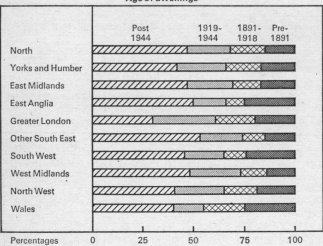

Age of dwellings

*Chart 7: Stock of dwellings
by region, tenure and age
England and Wales
December 1975*

Table 46

**Houses and flats completed
United Kingdom**

thousands

	Total	Local authorities and new towns	Other public sector[1]	Private owners
1945–55[2]	209·0	154·8	8·5	45·6
1956–60[2]	295·9	147·3	6·7	142·0
1961–65[2]	339·8	137·7	7·1	195·0
1966	396·0	176·9	10·5	208·6
1967	415·5	199·7	11·5	204·2
1968	425·8	188·0	11·8	226·1
1969	378·3	181·0	11·5	185·9
1970	362·2	176·9	11·0	174·3
1971	364·5	154·9	13·3	196·3
1972	330·9	120·4	9·8	200·8
1973	304·6	102·6	11·0	191·1
1974	279·6	121·0	13·4	145·2
1975	322·1	150·5	16·9	154·7
1976	324·1	151·7	17·7	154·8

1. Houses provided for the police, prison staffs, the armed forces, etc.
2. Average per year over each period.

Table 47

**Houses and flats completed
England and Wales**

	1966		1971		1976	
	Thousands	%	Thousands	%	Thousands	%
For local authorities and new towns						
Houses	69	48	55	47	70	56
Flats	74	52	62	53	54	44
All dwellings	142	100	117	100	124	100
For private owners						
Houses	180	91	167	93	123	89
Flats	18	9	13	7	15	11
All dwellings	198	100	180	100	138	100

Table 48

**Rents and mortgages
England and Wales**

£

	1966	1971	1976
Average weekly rents of accommodation			
Local authority owned[1]			
Greater London	2·06	3·48	5·38
Rest of England and Wales	1·51	2·35	4·23
Privately rented unfurnished (registered rents only)[2]			
Greater London	4·52	6·19	10·65
Rest of England and Wales	2·77	3·40	5·83
Average monthly mortgage repayments on new houses[3]			
Gross	26·23	40·40	112·70
Net in first year[4]	19·32	31·26	76·50

1. Average rebated rent in October, except in the case of tenants receiving supplementary benefit, where the rent is not rebated, since the full rent is taken into account when calculating entitlement to supplementary benefit.

2. First registrations excluding housing associations and decontrol cases.

3. Assuming 90 per cent of the average price of a new home advanced for 25 years at the interest rate recommended by the Building Societies Association at mid-year.

4. Allowing tax relief at the standard or basic rate on earned income.

Table 49

**Housing and land costs
England and Wales**

House prices   £

	1969	1971	1976
Average cost (including land) of new local authority dwellings			
England and Wales	4,190	5,140	12,090[3]
Greater London	6,280	7,450	..
Rest of England and Wales	3,840	4,550	..
Average price of new six-room[1] semi-detached houses sold (rounded to nearest £50)			
England and Wales	4,100	4,650	10,500
North	3,750	4,450	10,300
Yorkshire and Humberside	3,450	3,900	8,600
East Midlands	3,500	4,000	8,850
East Anglia	4,000	4,850	9,800
South East (including Greater London)	5,100	6,100	13,800
South West	4,150	4,850	11,200
West Midlands	3,950	4,350	10,400
North West	3,900	4,350	9,700
Wales	3,800	4,400	9,400

Land costs[2]   £ per plot

	1969	1971	1976
Weighted average price of private sector housing land			
England and Wales	828	1,030	1,848
North	301	495	1,006
Yorkshire and Humberside	401	420	1,174
East Midlands	555	687	1,088
East Anglia	530	604	1,260
Greater London	1,967	2,732	4,478
South East (excluding Greater London)	1,319	1,630	2,673
South West	582	788	1,727
West Midlands	1,014	1,081	1,986
North West	581	727	1,464
Wales	390	500	763

1. The 6 rooms are assumed to include 3 bedrooms.
2. Figures are for the standard regions as defined on 1 April 1974.
3. 1975 figure.

Table 50

**Slum clearance and house renovations
Great Britain**

thousands

	Houses demolished or closed		Renovation grants approved (dwellings)	
	England and Wales	Scotland	Local authorities	Private owners[1]
1945–55[2]	10·4	..	0·7[3]	8·9[3]
1956–60[2]	49·1	12·7	13·3	52·7
1961–65[2]	61·4	13·2	35·9	89·5
1966	66·8	16·7	33·7	81·6
1967	71·2	19·1	32·5	88·0
1968	71·6	18·8	40·9	87·0
1969	69·2	17·8	40·4	83·5
1970	67·8	17·3	59·5	120·5
1971	70·1	20·6	89·0	143·5
1972	66·1	18·5	136·9	231·2
1973	63·6	16·5	188·1	265·4
1974	41·7	11·6	121·3	179·1
1975	49·1	10·7	62·0	97·8
1976	48·2	6·8	74·7	94·0

1. Including housing associations.
2. Average per year over each period.
3. From 1949 in England and Wales and 1950 in Scotland.

Table 51

House conditions[1]
England[2]

	1971		1976	
	Thousand dwellings	%	Thousand dwellings	%
Total stock of dwellings	17,100	100	17,115	100
Amenities lacked:				
W.C. inside dwelling	2,032	12	1,083	6
Fixed bath in bathroom	1,630	10	800	5
Wash basin	2,043	12	991	6
Hot and cold water at 3 points	2,374	14	1,173	7
Sink	84	1	43	—
One or more of the above amenities	2,866	17	1,493	9
Unfit dwellings by tenure:				
Owner occupied	355	28	263	33
Rented from local authorities or new town corporations	58	5	46	6
Other tenures	645	52	334	42
Vacant	186	15	151	19
All unfit dwellings	1,244	100	794	100
Unfit dwellings by region:				
North, Yorkshire and Humberside and North West	540	43	382	48
South East	231	19	195	25
Rest of England[2]	473	38	217	27
All unfit dwellings	1,244	100	794	100

1. Figures obtained from the House Condition Survey.
2. 1971 figures are for England and Wales.

Table 52

**Homeless households:
by type of last accommodation
and by reason for loss of
accommodation
England**

percentages

	London			Rest of England			England		
	1975		1976	1975		1976	1975		1976
	half years			half years			half years		
	1	2	1	1	2	1	1	2	1
Type of last accommodation:									
Living with friends/ relations	37	35	35	32	29	29	34	31	31
Owner occupied	6	7	7	14	15	17	11	12	13
Local or public authority	7	9	11	10	12	12	9	11	12
Rented: private unfurnished	9	7	8	9	9	9	9	8	9
private furnished	22	22	18	11	10	10	15	15	14
Housing association	1	1	1	—	—	1	1	1	1
Tied accommodation/rent free	7	6	6	15	16	15	12	12	11
Squat	5	7	7	1	1	1	2	3	3
All other tenures	7	6	8	9	8	7	8	7	7
Reason for loss of accommodation:									
Dispute: husband/wife/ cohabitee	8	9	9	13	12	13	11	11	11
other relatives	22	21	22	20	20	19	21	20	20
other	8	8	7	7	8	7	7	8	7
Rent arrears	6	7	8	6	7	7	6	7	7
Illegal letting/ unauthorized occupancy	5	5	5	3	3	4	4	4	4
Landlord requires/ repossessed	18	15	13	10	10	9	12	12	11
All other cases	34	35	36	41	40	41	38	38	40
Total homeless households (=100%) (thousands)	6·3	6·3	6·4	11·0	10·0	10·7	17·2	16·4	17·2

Table 53

**Transport of goods and passengers
Great Britain**

	Unit	1966	1971	1976
Goods transport				
Total tonnes	Million	1,950	1,889	1,686
Road	"	1,641	1,582	1,420[2]
Rail	"	217	198	176
Coastal shipping	"	53	47	39
British waterways	"	8	6	5
Oil pipelines	"	31	56	46
Total tonne/kilometres	Thousand million	124·5	135·0	136·4
Road	"	73·3	85·9	90·0[2]
Rail	"	24·2	24·3	23·1
Coastal shipping	"	25·3	21·4	20·0
British waterways	"	0·2	0·1	0·1
Oil pipelines	"	1·5	3·3	3·2
Passenger transport				
Total passenger kilometres	Thousand million	347·6	420·1	447·4
Air (domestic services)[1]	"	1·8	2·0	2·3
Rail	"	34·6	35·4	33·0
Road:				
Public service vehicles	"	62·0	56·0	53·0[2]
Private transport	"	249·2	326·7	359·1

1. Including Northern Ireland and the Channel Islands.
2. Provisional.

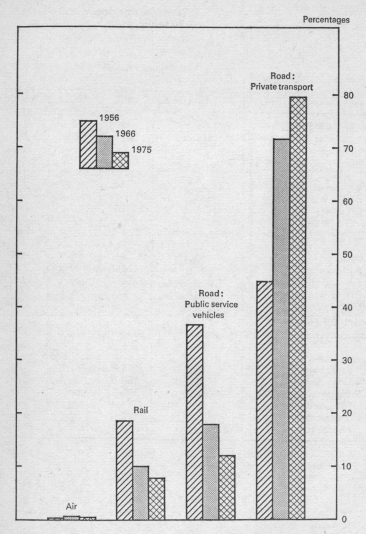

Percentages

Road:
Private transport

1956
1966
1975

Road:
Public service
vehicles

Rail

Air

***Chart 8: Shares of total
passenger mileage
Great Britain***

Table 54

Cost of passenger transport to consumers

Index numbers of prices, 1970 = 100

	1966	1971	1976
Railway fares	82	116	261
Bus and coach stage service fares	76	118	238
Prices of new and second-hand cars and motor cycles	84	108	205
Running cost of motor vehicles	82	106	216

Table 55

London commuter traffic

Passenger traffic entering Central London[1] during the morning peak 07.00 to 10.00 hours

persons (thousands)

	1966[2]	1971	1975	Percentage change 1966–75
Total all transport	1,213	1,165	1,075	−11·3
Public transport	1,047	991	895	−14·6
British Rail	456	460	403	−11·6
London Transport rail[3]	416	385	344	−17·4
London Transport bus	175	146	148	−15·4
Private transport	166	174	181	+ 9·0
Private car	142	163	162	+13·9
Motorcycle/cycle	24	12	19	−20·5

1. This area approximates to that defined as the Greater London Conurbation Centre in the Population Census of 1961. It is bounded by South Kensington and Paddington in the west, Marylebone Road/Euston Road in the north, Shoreditch and Aldgate in the east and Elephant & Castle and Vauxhall in the south.
2. Estimated.
3. Adjusted to allow for double counting of passengers transferring between British Rail and London Transport rail services.

Table 56

**Road transport
Great Britain**

Length of surfaced[1] road

At 1 April   kilometres

	1966	1971	1976
Total road length	314,623	324,665	333,418
Motorways	631	1,270	2,226
Trunk roads	13,415	13,433	13,488
Principal roads[2]	32,039	32,702	33,134
Other roads	268,538	277,260	284,570

1. Unsurfaced roads (greenlanes) are not included. At 1 April 1974 these comprised about 12,000 kilometres.
2. Class 1 roads in 1966.

Road expenditure

£ million

	1966/67	1971/72	1975/76
Total expenditure on highways	466·3	844·5	1,527·0
New construction and improvement[1]	214·6	504·4	800·3
Trunk roads and motorways	119·3	241·2	462·0
Principal roads[2]	} 95·3	197·1	257·3
Other roads		66·1	80·9
Maintenance[1,3]	160·5	190·0	359·3
Trunk roads and motorways	22·7	30·7	63·3
Principal roads[2]	} 137·8	40·9	76·1
Other roads		118·4	220·0
Cleansing, gritting and snow clearing[3]	23·4	38·2	59·1
Principal roads[2]	} 23·4	8·3	11·2
Other roads		29·9	47·9
Other expenditure[4]	..	..	48·8
Public lighting	31·7	40·4	84·6
Car parks	5·5	10·8	16·5
Administration	30·6	60·7	158·3

1. Minor improvements included with maintenance in 1966/67.
2. Class I roads in 1966.
3. Trunk road and motorway cleansing, etc. included with maintenance.
4. Includes depots, plant, vehicles and equipment for which the corresponding expenditure in 1966/67 and 1971/72 was spread over the preceding items in the table.

Table 57

**Motor vehicles currently licensed
United Kingdom**

thousands

	1966	1971	1976
All motor vehicles	13,621	15,859	18,214
Private cars and private vans	9,747	12,361	14,355
Motor cycles, scooters and mopeds	1,430	1,033	1,235
Public transport vehicles	96	108	115
Goods vehicles	1,611	1,660	1,795
Agricultural tractors, etc.	478	450	414
Other vehicles	97	103	121
Crown and exempt vehicles	163	144	180

Table 58

**Estimated traffic on all roads
Great Britain**

thousand million vehicle kilometres

	1966	1971	1976
All motor vehicles	172·84	220·48	251·44
Cars and taxis[1]	126·51	173·92	200·53
Two-wheeled motor vehicles	5·97	3·80	5·80
Mopeds	1·06	0·69	0·95
Motor scooters	1·82	0·99	0·49
Motor cycles	3·09	2·13	4·37
Buses and coaches	3·89	3·60	3·52
Total goods vehicles	36·48	39·16	41·58
Light vans[2]	18·03	19·69	21·36
Other goods vehicles	18·45	19·47	20·22
Pedal cycles	6·25	4·11	3·93

1. Includes three-wheeled cars.
2. Not exceeding 30 cwt unladen weight.

Table 59

**Traffic on all roads by vehicle
and road class, 1976
Great Britain**

thousand million vehicle kilometres

	All roads	Motorways	Urban	Rural
All motor vehicles	251·44	23·40	122·01	106·02
Cars and taxis	200·53	17·31	99·40	83·82
Motor cycles	5·80	0·09	3·53	2·18
Buses and coaches	3·52	0·24	2·00	1·28
Light vans	21·36	1·40	10·55	9·41
Other goods vehicles	20·22	4·36	6·52	9·33

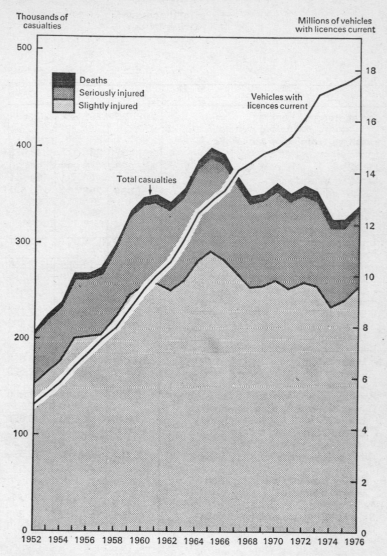

Thousands of
casualties

Millions of vehicles
with licences current

500

18

■ Deaths
▨ Seriously injured
░ Slightly injured

Vehicles with
licences current

16

400

14

Total casualties

300

12

10

200

8

6

100

4

2

0   0
1952 1954 1956 1958 1960 1962 1964 1966 1968 1970 1972 1974 1976

**Chart 9: Casualties in road
accidents
Great Britain**

Table 60
Road accidents
Great Britain

	1966	1971	1976
Road accidents (number)	291,725	258,727	258,639
Casualties from road accidents (number)	392,457	352,027	339,673
Killed	7,985	7,699	6,570
Seriously injured	99,838	90,868	79,531
Slightly injured	284,634	253,460	253,572
Persons killed or seriously injured			
By class of road user: (number)			
Total all ages	107,823	98,567	86,101
Pedestrians			
Under 15	10,603	11,055	7,866
15 and over	17,151	15,479	12,715
Unknown	185	3	49
Pedal cyclists			
Under 15	2,508	2,513	2,124
15 and over	4,635	3,105	2,803
Unknown	76	2	4
Riders of 2-wheeled motor vehicles			
Under 20	10,298	7,120	10,058
20 and over	8,817	6,311	7,823
Unknown	263	3	20
Passengers on 2-wheeled motor vehicles	3,338	2,148	1,950
Drivers of 4-wheeled motor vehicles			
Under 25	7,845	8,526	6,886
25 and over	15,935	17,795	15,242
Unknown	412	9	31
Other passengers	25,757	24,498	18,530
By class of road user per 100 million vehicle kilometres:			
Pedal cyclists	115	137	126
Riders of 2-wheeled motor vehicles	325	353	308
Drivers of other motor vehicles	14	12	9
Cars and taxis	15	13	10
Goods vehicles	12	9	6
Public service vehicles	3	3	4

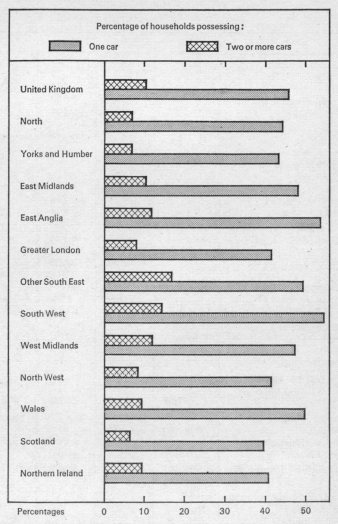

**Chart 10: Vehicle ownership
by region, average of 1974 and 1975
United Kingdom**

Table 61

Rail transport
Great Britain

	Unit	1966	1971	1976
Route open for passenger traffic				
British Rail	Kilometres	18,359	14,484	14,407
London Transport	"	344	388	381
Other railways	"	80	104	184[5]
Stations				
British Rail	Number	3,803	2,820	2,865
Passenger and freight	"	582	218	—
Passenger (including parcels)	"	2,306	2,213	2,378
Freight	"	915	389	487
London Transport	"	228	248	248
Other railways	"	48	63	82[5]
Rolling stock (British Rail)[1]				
Locomotives – total	Number	6,991	4,124	3,689
steam	"	1,689	—	—
diesel	"	4,962	3,806	3,338
electric	"	340	318	351
Passenger carriages[2]	Thousands	22·5	18·3	17·1
Non-passenger vehicles	"	7·4	6·2	5·3
Freight vehicles	"	551·4	303·4	191·2
Passenger receipts				
British Rail	£ million	179·4	261·0	505·1
London Transport	"	39·1	62·6	121·9
Other railways	"	0·6	1·0	1·9[5]
Freight receipts (British Rail including mails and parcels)	£ million	275·2	258·9	405·2
Passenger journeys				
British Rail	Millions	835	816	708
London Transport	"	667	654	546
Other railways	"	24	17	9[5]
Freight traffic (British Rail)	Million tonnes	217·0	198·3	177·7[4]
Rail accidents (all railways)				
persons killed[3]	Number	125	125	93
persons injured[3]	"	13,591	12,333	10,326

1. Excludes small gauge stock.
2. Including the following multiple unit power cars: 5,403 (1966); 4,897 (1971); 4,677 (1976).
3. Excludes casualties from incidents involving trespassers, suicides and attempted suicides.
4. Includes 1·4 million tonnes of mails and parcels.   5. Provisional.

Table 62

**Users' expenditure on inland transport
United Kingdom**

£ million

	1966	1971	1976
Passenger			
Buses and coaches	399	522	1,058
Motoring	2,402	4,182	8,936
Taxis and hire car	57	125	215
Rail	222	329	634
Total	3,080	5,158	10,843
Freight			
Road	2,812	4,589	9,501
Rail	281	267	415
Total	3,093	4,856	9,916
Inland waterways			
Total	3	2	4
All inland transport	6,178	10,016	20,763
of which			
Road	5,670	9,418	19,710
Rail	503	596	1,049
Motoring			
Purchase of vehicle	917	1,628	3,190
Petrol	724	1,293	3,208
Oil	41	68	94
Repairs, servicing, replacements and other motor-vehicle cost	413	694	1,469
Insurance	60	78	187
Vehicle tests	4	15	35
Vehicle and driving licences	179	320	600
Driving tests	2	5	9
Driving lessons	21	23	50
Garage rents and parking	41	58	94
All expenditure	2,402	4,182	8,936
of which			
Consumers' expenditure	1,791	3,311	6,917
Business expenditure	611	871	2,019

Table 63
Air transport
All UK airlines

	Unit	1966	1971	1976
Fleets				
Aircraft in service at end of June	Number	375	415	505
Passenger traffic				
Passengers carried on scheduled and charter services	Thousands	15,237	23,398	27,507
Passenger-kilometres flown	Millions	19,498	34,966	49.133
Revenue traffic[1]				
Domestic services				
Aircraft stage flights				
Number	Number	141,257	149,839	155,884
Average length	Kilometres	282	273	299
Aircraft-kilometres flown	Thousands	39,840	40,887	46,654
Passengers carried	"	5,123	5,367	6,147
Passenger-kilometres flown	Millions	1,845	1,972	2,326
Cargo carried – Total	Tonnes	77,148	58,338	46,078
International services				
Aircraft stage flights				
Number	Number	210,342	214,087	208,888
Average length	Kilometres	910	1,239	1,218
Aircraft-kilometres flown	Thousands	191,495	265,168	254,379
Passengers carried	"	6,936	9,095	11,323
Passenger-kilometres flown	Millions	11,505	16,692	28,752
Cargo carried – Total	Tonnes	271,774	191,737	201,608

1. Scheduled services only. Including services of UK Airways Corporations and private companies but not those of the Corporations' associates and subsidiaries overseas.

Table 64
Use of UK airports

	1966	1971	1976
Air transport movements (thousands)			
Total	556	630	740
UK operators			
Scheduled	378	362	413
Non-scheduled	49	107	153
Foreign operators			
Scheduled	118	145	150
Non-scheduled	11	17	24
Terminal passengers (millions)			
Total	22·6	34·9	44·7
UK operators			
Scheduled	14·4	16·9	21·7
Non-scheduled	2·6	8·4	8·9
Foreign operators			
Scheduled	5·0	8·2	11·9
Non-scheduled	0·6	1·5	2·2

Table 65
Aircraft noise
Heathrow airport

	1966	1971	1976
Number of day jet departures (thousands)	56	107	123
Percentage exceeding the permitted noise level of 110 PNdB	0·7	0·3	1·85
Number of night jet departures (thousands)	3·5	4·1	2·4
Percentage exceeding the permitted noise level of 102 PNdB	2·8	1·6	11·1

Table 66
Accidents on scheduled
passenger carrying services
UK airways[1]

	1965 to 1969	1970 to 1974	1972	1973	1974	1975	1976
Fatal accidents	6	2	1	—	—	—	1
Passenger casualties:							
killed	273	167	112	—	—	—	54
seriously injured	2	5	3	—	—	4	—
Crew casualties:							
killed	32	14	6	—	—	—	9
seriously injured	2	2	—	1	1	—	—
Passengers carried per passenger killed (thousands)	222·2	466·3	502·0				
Passenger miles flown per passenger killed (thousands)	158·6	408·7	495·5				

1. Services of UK Airways Corporations and private companies but not those of the Corporations' associates and subsidiaries overseas.

Table 67

Shipping:
UK merchant vessels in service

500 gross tons and over

At end of year

	1966	1971	1976
Number			
All vessels	2,319	1,875	1,573
Passenger[1]	191	122	104
Dry cargo	1,637	1,257	1,046
Tankers	491	496	423
Thousand gross tons			
All vessels	20,522	25,177	29,839
Passenger[1]	1,971	1,101	661
Dry cargo	10,694	10,771	13,437
Tankers	7,857	13,304	15,742
Thousand deadweight tons			
All vessels	26,931	38,955	49,313
Passenger[1]	1,052	478	205
Dry cargo	14,005	15,101	20,463
Tankers	11,874	23,376	28,645

1. All vessels with passenger certificates.

Table 68

International seaborne trade
of the United Kingdom, 1976

Proportion of trade carried by the
principal flags

percentage

	Imports		Exports	
	Weight	Value	Weight	Value
Country of flag				
United Kingdom	32	41	45	49
Liberia	17	6	3	1
Norway	9	5	6	3
Greece	5	2	6	3
Germany (FR)	6	10	8	9
Netherlands	6	6	6	6
Other EEC flags	8	11	9	11
All other flags	17	19	17	18

Table 69

Trade with deep-sea and near and short-sea areas[1] by port

thousand tonnes

	1966		1971		1975	
	Imp.	Exp.	Imp.	Exp.	Imp.	Exp.
Trade with deep-sea areas						
Northern	2,530	680	3,876	861	3,567	666
Yorkshire and Humberside	2,793	160	2,959	579	5,206	746
East Midlands	12	1	9	—	15	4
East Anglia	140	44	400	200	618	512
South East	7,710	2,313	8,002	3,171	6,344	3,621
South West	2,472	301	2,246	133	1,499	147
North West	9,455	3,361	7,775	3,612	5,004	2,929
Wales	3,907	795	6,662	816	3,186	382
Scotland	3,587	577	3,948	909	3,063	690
Northern Ireland	1,078	24	1,380	20	427	10
Trade with near and short-sea areas						
Northern	4,069	815	4,245	1,179	4,233	1,738
Yorkshire and Humberside	4,369	1,441	5,795	1,757	6,885	2,668
East Midlands	310	170	462	91	488	140
East Anglia	1,618	903	3,113	2,104	4,673	3,320
South East	7,823	2,394	8,616	2,947	9,704	3,890
South West	1,021	2,038	1,442	2,622	2,124	2,765
North West	4,479	1,598	3,732	1,979	3,963	2,062
Wales	4,688	1,054	2,734	1,631	2,943	1,323
Scotland	3,373	729	3,303	840	3,247	1,182
Northern Ireland	658	127	719	180	1,160	180

1. Excluding fuels.

Table 70

**Postal, telegraph and telephone services
United Kingdom**

	Unit	1966	1971	1976
Year ended 31 March				
Letters, etc. posted[1]	Millions	11,300	10,500	9,903
Parcels posted	„	230	177	165
Money orders handled[2]	„	16	10	3
Postal orders issued	„	674	435	225
Telegrams[3]	„	32	26	21
Telephone calls (inland)	„	6,892	10,747	16,092
At 31 March				
Length of telephone wire	Million kms	73	108	142
Private telephone stations	Thousands	10,546	14,782	20,806
Public call offices	„	75	76	78
Telephone exchanges[4]	Number	6,036	6,168	6,263
Telex stations	„	17,092	32,945	59,421

1. Including printed papers, newspapers, postcards and sample packets.
2. Inland, Commonwealth and foreign.
3. Inland and foreign via the Post Office system, but excluding those sent abroad via the private cable companies' system.
4. Excluding automanual and trunk exchanges.

Table 71
Rainfall

millimetres

	England		Wales	
	Average 1916–1950	1976	Average 1916–1950	1976
Annual total	832	733	1,357	1,145
January	83	54	149	104
February	60	35	105	80
March	52	38	85	77
April	57	20	82	28
May	59	59	86	91
June	52	16	79	28
July	75	31	106	35
August	75	27	116	20
September	69	145	114	242
October	83	142	148	202
November	88	78	145	121
December	79	88	142	117
	Scotland		Northern Ireland	
	Average 1916–1950	1976	Average 1916–1950	1976
Annual total	1,419	1,314	1,081	1,008
January	154	185	109	126
February	106	87	76	51
March	89	130	66	81
April	88	60	67	30
May	87	118	72	112
June	87	65	71	55
July	114	64	96	59
August	122	25	102	16
September	128	141	96	121
October	158	202	111	191
November	143	127	104	68
December	143	110	111	98

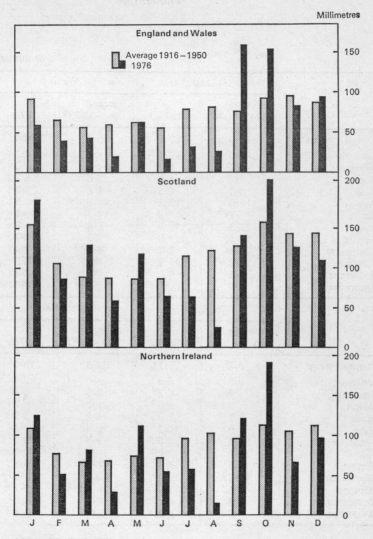

Chart 11: Rainfall

Table 72

Temperature

Daily mean air temperature at
sea level

degrees centigrade

	England and Wales		Wales	
	Average 1941–1970	1976	Average 1941–1970	1976
Annual mean	10·0	10·5	10·2	10·4
January	4·0	6·2	4·6	6·7
February	4·2	5·0	4·6	5·0
March	6·2	5·4	6·5	5·8
April	8·8	8·3	8·8	8·5
May	11·6	12·2	11·6	11·9
June	14·7	17·1	14·3	16·1
July	16·3	18·5	15·8	17·8
August	16·1	17·6	15·7	17·7
September	14·3	13·8	14·1	13·4
October	11·2	11·2	11·3	10·7
November	7·2	6·8	7·7	7·4
December	5·1	2·8	5·9	3·6
	Scotland		Northern Ireland	
	Average 1941–1970	1976	Average 1941–1970	1976
Annual mean	8·7	9·1	9·3	9·4
January	3·5	5·0	4·0	5·8
February	3·7	5·2	4·3	5·3
March	5·4	4·9	6·2	5·7
April	7·5	7·8	8·2	8·3
May	9·9	10·2	10·8	10·6
June	12·7	13·9	13·5	15·3
July	14·1	16·1	14·7	16·2
August	14·0	15·3	14·6	16·1
September	12·5	12·2	13·0	12·6
October	9·9	9·8	10·4	9·2
November	6·3	6·2	6·7	5·8
December	4·6	2·2	5·0	2·4

Degrees centigrade

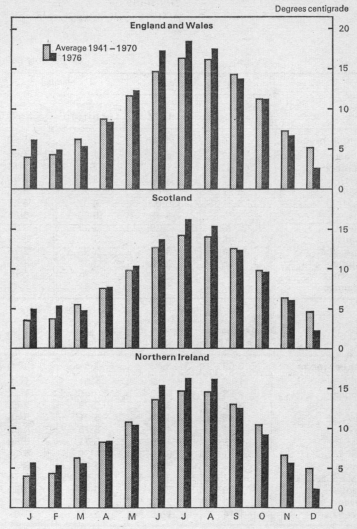

Chart 12: Temperature

Table 73
Sunshine

mean hours per day

	England and Wales		Wales	
	Average 1941–1970	1976	Average 1941–1970	1976
Annual mean	4·04	4·40	3·86	3·90
January	1·59	1·67	1·52	1·19
February	2·43	1·73	2·39	2·15
March	3·67	3·56	3·70	3·26
April	5·27	5·43	5·25	5·25
May	6·31	5·62	6·07	4·92
June	6·79	8·49	6·45	6·84
July	5·38	8·29	5·42	6·45
August	5·48	8·33	5·17	8·07
September	4·44	3·60	3·98	2·75
October	3·25	2·18	2·88	2·16
November	1·94	2·17	1·74	2·14
December	1·47	1·85	1·31	1·57

	Scotland		Northern Ireland	
	Average 1941–1970	1976	Average 1941–1970	1976
Annual mean	3·53	3·53	3·54	3·50
January	1·40	1·12	1·51	1·21
February	2·53	1·72	2·45	1·74
March	3·36	3·02	3·29	2·53
April	4·99	4·24	5·01	5·46
May	5·74	4·48	6·15	4·00
June	5·79	4·86	5·71	5·88
July	4·81	6·40	4·36	4·14
August	4·48	7·35	4·52	8·05
September	3·71	3·01	3·58	3·19
October	2·70	2·38	2·66	2·50
November	1·73	2·28	1·95	2·36
December	1·14	1·46	1·20	1·01

Table 74

Area of the United Kingdom, 1976

thousand hectares

	Total	Land	Inland water[1]
United Kingdom	24,411	24,104	307
Great Britain	22,999	22,756	243
England and Wales	15,121	15,039	83
England	13,045	12,975	70
Wales	2,077	2,064	13
Scotland	7,877	7,717	160
Northern Ireland[2]	1,412	1,348	64

square kilometres

	Total	Land	Inland water[1]
United Kingdom	244,108	241,042	3,066
Great Britain	229,988	227,559	2,429
England and Wales	151,213	150,388	825
England	130,447	129,747	699
Wales	20,766	20,640	126
Scotland	78,775	77,170	1,604
Northern Ireland[2]	14,120	13,483	637

1. Excluding tidal water.
2. Excluding certain tidal waters that are parts of statutory areas in Northern Ireland.

Table 75

Water supply
Availability and consumption
by Water Authority area, 1974
United Kingdom

thousand cubic metres per day[1]

	Portable water		Area population (millions)
	Net total available	Supply consumed	
Water Authority area			
North West	2,347	903	7·1
Northumbrian	779	335	2·7
Severn–Trent	2,137	751	8·2
Yorkshire	1,306	429	4·5
Anglian	1,443	596	4·6
Thames	3,196	794	11·8
Southern	1,055	338	3·8
Wessex	687	224	2·3
South West	382	104	1·3
Welsh National Water Development Authority	1,017	320	3·0
United Kingdom			
England and Wales	14,397	4,794	49·2
Scotland[2]	2,139	744	5·2
Northern Ireland[2]	538	157	1·5

1. Averages per day over the year.
2. 1973 data.

Table 76

Forest area
United Kingdom

	At 31 March		thousand hectares
	1966	1971	1976
Forest area			
United Kingdom	1,829	1,908	2,043
Great Britain	1,785	1,853	1,980
Forestry Commission			
Productive	647	727	826
Unproductive	39	24	23
Private Woodlands			
Productive	747	768	846
Unproductive	352	334	285
Northern Ireland[1]	44[2]	55[2]	63[2]
Forestry Commission in Great Britain			
Total estates	1,104	1,212	1,231
Land under plantation	647	727	826
Plantable land acquired	14·0	21·4	19·4
Total area planted[3]	21·8	28·5	20·5
Area lost by fire	0·2	0·2	0·3
State afforestation in Northern Ireland[1]			
Total estates	53·6	62·2	67·0
Land under plantation	32·6	42·1	49·2
Plantable land acquired	1·2	0·8	1·1
Total area planted[4]	2·1	1·6	1·2
Area lost by fire	—	0·036	0·1

1. 1966 figures are at 30 September.
2. Includes unproductive woodland.
3. Including replanting after damage by fire.
4. Including areas replanted.

Table 77

**Air pollution by region
United Kingdom**

	1972/73	1974/75	1975/76
Smoke: average concentration[1]			
England			
North	74	37	34
Yorkshire and Humberside	65	38	43
East Midlands	55	35	36
East Anglia	40	25	25
South East (excluding Greater			
London)	27	19	22
Greater London	36	28	34
South West	26	19	21
West Midlands	48	37	38
North West	65	39	37
Wales	29	23	22
Scotland	49	32	26
Northern Ireland	50	38	46

1. Measured in micrograms per cubic metre.

Table 78

**River pollution
England and Wales
1973**

kilometres

	Non-tidal rivers	Tidal rivers	Canals
Total miles	35,942	2,873	2,479
Chemical classification			
Unpolluted	28,095	1,455	1,189
Doubtful	5,064	641	921
Poor	1,506	419	243
Grossly polluted	1,277	358	126

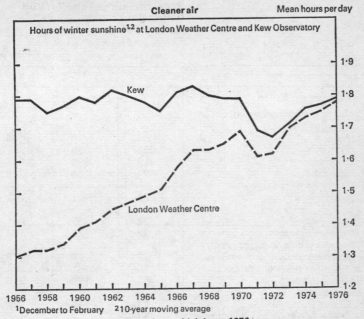

Cleaner air — Mean hours per day

Hours of winter sunshine[1,2] at London Weather Centre and Kew Observatory

[1]December to February [2]10-year moving average

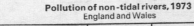

Pollution of non-tidal rivers, 1973
England and Wales

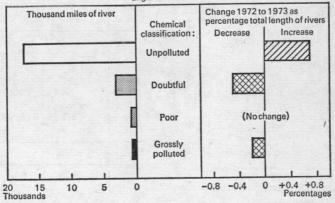

*Chart 13: Cleaner air and
non-tidal river pollution
England and Wales*

Table 79

Government expenditure on education
United Kingdom

£ million

	1966/67	1971/72	1976/77
Current expenditure			
Schools maintained by education authorities:			
Nursery	4	8	34
Primary	369	639	1,735
Secondary	413	699	2,024
Special	23	55	209
Total	809	1,401	4,002
School health[1]	22	37	—
Transport of pupils	22	43	100
Fees and grants to direct grant and independent schools	33	48	113
Further and adult education	188	351	944
Teacher training	68	129	296
Universities:			
Grants to universities	139	259	639
Grants and allowances to students	53	77	152
Youth service and physical training	15	27	82
Administrative and other expenses	102	161	359
Total current expenditure	1,451	2,533	6,687
Capital expenditure			
Schools	169	327	517
Further and adult education	39	64	81
Teacher training	12	12	10
Grants to universities	82	81	104
Other capital expenditure	1	9	24
Total capital expenditure	303	493	736
Total expenditure			
Central government	308	483	1,012
Local authorities	1,446	2,543	6,411
Total government expenditure	1,754	3,026	7,423

1. From 1 April 1974 expenditure on the school health service is included in the national health service.

Table 80

**Schools, teachers and pupils
United Kingdom**

	At January		thousands
	1966	1971	1976
England and Wales			
All schools			
Schools and departments	34	33	33
Full-time teachers	335	385	476
Pupils on registers			
Nursery 2–4 years[1]	271	351	522
Infant 5–6 years	1,471	1,658	1,520
Junior[2]	2,951	3,389	3,497
Secondary up to 15 years[3]	2,403	2,586	2,960
aged 15 and over	782	890	1,334
Scotland			
All schools			
Schools and departments	3·3	3·6	3·7[4]
Full-time teachers	39·8	45·8	56·3[4]
Pupils on registers			
Nursery[1]	8·3	13·8	23·7[4]
Infant	188·7	193·9	173·2[4]
Primary	420·9	450·5	463·0[4]
Secondary up to 15 years	220·8	244·3	266·9[4]
aged 15 and over	71·2	91·3	153·8[4]
Special schools	11·3	12·5	13·1[4]
Northern Ireland			
Grant-aided schools			
Schools and departments	1·7	1·5	1·4
Full-time teachers	12·1	14·5	17·1
Pupils on registers			
Nursery 2–4 years[1]	0·6	1·0	1·8
Infant } 4–11 years Primary }	191·4	217·8	216·7
Secondary 11–15 years	99·4	112·9	129·6
aged 16 and over	12·7	18·0	22·7

1. Full-time and part-time.
2. 7–10 years and $\frac{1}{3}$ 11-year-olds.
3. $\frac{2}{3}$ 11-year-olds and 12–14 years.
4. As at September 1975.

Table 81

**Schools, teachers and pupils –
detailed analysis
England and Wales**

	At January		number
	1966	1971	1976
Maintained primary schools[1]			
Pupils on registers:			
Full-time	4,366,372	5,023,130	5,048,370
Part-time	11,382	37,547	116,763
Full-time teachers[2]	147,373	176,676	203,139
Full-time equivalent of part-time			
teachers[2]	8,571	10,905	10,599
Pupils per teacher	28·0	26·9	23·9
Maintained secondary schools[1]			
Full-time pupils on registers	2,816,793	3,143,879	3,935,500
Full-time teachers[2]	143,627	164,618	221,287
Full-time equivalent of part-time			
teachers[2]	9,691	10,604	9,789
Pupils per teacher	18·4	17·9	17·0
All schools	33,582	32,714	33,100
Maintained			
Primary	22,822	22,936	22,685
Middle deemed primary	•	118	645
Middle deemed secondary	•	147	509
Secondary – all schools	5,798	5,148	4,473
Modern	3,642	2,464	1,002
Grammar	1,273	970	477
Technical	150	67	23
Comprehensive	387	1,373	2,878
Other	346	274	93
Immigrant centres	•	19	23
Grant-aided nursery	477	512	636
All special schools	902	1,019	1,619
Direct grant grammar	179	176	170
Other direct grant	6	3	4
Independent			
Recognized as efficient	1,538	1,402	1,358
Other	1,860	1,234	978

1. In 1971 and 1976 immigrant centres and middle schools deemed primary are included with primary schools; middle schools deemed secondary are included with secondary schools.
2. 1966 figures show all teachers; 1971 and 1976 figures show qualified teachers only.

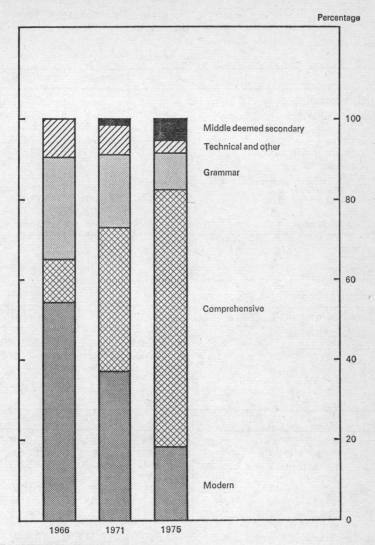

Percentage

Middle deemed secondary

Technical and other

Grammar

Comprehensive

Modern

1966   1971   1975

*Chart 14: Pupils in public
sector secondary schools
England and Wales*

Table 82

Pupil/teacher ratios, 1976
United Kingdom

At January

	Primary	Secondary
Public sector schools		
England and Wales	23·9	17·0
North	23·0	17·0
Yorkshire and Humberside	23·5	17·5
East Midlands	24·7	17·1
East Anglia	23·7	17·7
Greater London	22·6	16·3
Rest of the South East	24·2	17·1
South West	24·7	17·5
West Midlands	24·8	16·8
North West	24·4	16·9
Wales	22·8	17·1
Scotland[1]	22·4	15·1
Northern Ireland	26·3	17·0

1. At September 1975.

Table 83

Maintained special schools
England and Wales

At January

	1966	1971	1976
Schools – Total	778	905	1,505
Day	547	635	1,180
Boarding	231	270	325
Pupils – Total	67,416	81,733	124,836
Day	54,239	67,397	110,344
Boarding	13,177	14,336	14,492
Full-time teachers[1]	5,840	7,817	14,337
Men	2,480	3,400	4,851
Women	3,360	4,417	9,486
Pupils per teacher	11·5	10·5	8·7

1. Including full-time equivalent of part-time teachers. All teachers in 1966 and 1971. Qualified teachers only in 1976.

Table 84

Distribution of pupils in classes of various sizes in public sector schools England and Wales

At January   percentages

	1966	1971	1976
Primary (as registered)[1]			
Percentage of full-time pupils in classes of size:			
1–15	1·1	0·9	1·2
16–20	3·1	2·6	3·7
21–25	6·7	6·3	11·6
26–30	14·0	17·3	29·9
31–35	25·5	35·7	37·1
36–40	34·2	32·6	15·0
41 and over	15·4	4·5	1·5
Thousands of pupils (=100%)	4,366	4,987	4,828
All middle (as taught)			
Percentage of pupils in classes of size:			
1–15	·	3·0	3·8
16–20	·	4·8	6·1
21–25	·	8·0	12·2
26–30	·	26·9	29·6
31–35	·	33·0	31·3
36–40	·	18·3	9·0
41 and over	·	6·0	7·9
Thousands of pupils (=100%)	·	91	442[2]
Secondary (as taught)			
Percentage of pupils in classes of size:			
1–15	9·3	11·3	11·5
16–20	11·8	12·6	14·4
21–25	13·9	13·9	17·4
26–30	25·4	27·2	30·7
31–35	27·4	25·6	18·5
36–40	9·2	4·5	1·7
41 and over	3·1	4·9	5·8
Thousands of pupils (=100%)	2,764[3]	3,016[4]	3,623[5]

1. Including immigrant centres in 1971 and 1976.
2. Excluding 603 pupils not in classes.
3. Excluding 53 thousand pupils not in classes.
4. Excluding 72 thousand pupils not in classes.
5. Excluding 90 thousand pupils not in classes.

Table 85

**Education beyond compulsory
school leaving age
England and Wales**

	1973/74		1975/76[1]	
	Men	Women	Men	Women
Total population aged 16–17 (thousands)	720	682	754	715
Students aged 16–17 as a percentage of population:				
Schools[2]	35·4	35·1	35·7	35·5
Further education:				
Full-time and sandwich courses	6·2	8·5	8·3	11·3
Part-time day courses	22·1	6·6	18·6	6·0
Evening only courses (major establishments)	4·6	7·0	3·6	6·4
Evening institutes	8·6	8·1	8·2	8·6
All students	76·6	65·4	74·5	67·8
Total population aged 18–20 (thousands)	1,047	989	1,070	1,013
Students aged 18–20 as a percentage of population:				
Schools	2·7	2·1	2·7	2·1
Further education:				
Full-time and sandwich courses	6·1	4·0	6·9	5·1
Part-time day courses	18·0	3·0	18·4	3·5
Evening only courses (major establishments)	4·4	5·0	3·9	5·2
Evening institutes	4·2	5·8	4·6	7·3
Initial teacher training courses (not included elsewhere)[3]	1·2	4·7	0·9	3·6
Universities[4]	6·5	3·8	6·7	4·0
All students	43·2	28·3	44·1	30·9

1. Provisional.
2. Including those of the 16 age group under school leaving age.
3. Formerly colleges of education.
4. Excluding part-time students.

Table 86

Pupils aged 17 in maintained schools – by region
England and Wales

At January   percentages

	1966[1]	1971[1]	1976[2,3]
England and Wales			
Boys	13·4	18·1	18·4
Girls	11·4	17·4	18·8
North			
Boys	10·3	15·5	16·0
Girls	9·0	15·3	15·5
Yorkshire and Humberside			
Boys	12·7	17·6	17·0
Girls	10·5	16·4	17·0
East Midlands			
Boys	11·8	16·1	16·4
Girls	9·8	14·5	16·1
East Anglia			
Boys	10·9	14·9	14·9
Girls	8·7	13·4	14·4
South East[4]			
Boys	16·1	21·6	22·6
Girls	13·2	20·7	23·2
South West			
Boys	13·2	18·3	16·8
Girls	11·4	17·0	16·8
West Midlands			
Boys	11·2	15·3	16·6
Girls	9·6	15·0	17·4
North West			
Boys	10·6	14·3	14·5
Girls	9·8	14·6	15·3
Wales			
Boys	17·4	21·5	20·3
Girls	17·2	21·4	21·8

1. Pupils aged 17 expressed as a percentage of the 13-year-old pupils 4 years earlier.

2. Pupils aged 17 expressed as a percentage of 14-year-old pupils 3 years earlier.

3. The percentages for 1976 relate to the regions as they exist following the local government reorganization which took place on 1 April 1974. Thus, with the exception of East Anglia and Wales, these percentages are not comparable with earlier years.

4. Including the Greater London Area.

Table 87

School leavers' certificate of education achievements England and Wales

	1966/67	1971/72	1975/76[1]
All leavers (thousands)	594·8	644·7	707·4
General Certificate of Education[2]			
Percentage of leavers who:			
Attempted Ordinary level	39·3	42·6	51·2
Obtained 1 or more 'O' level passes	39·6	37·8	37·3
Obtained 3 or more 'O' level passes	29·5	28·3	26·9
Obtained 5 or more 'O' level passes	22·2	21·1	19·5
Attempted Advanced Level	16·6	18·4	17·9
Obtained 1 or more 'A' level passes	14·8	16·2	15·9
Obtained 2 or more 'A' level passes	11·8	12·7	12·8
Certificate of Secondary Education[3]			
Percentage of leavers who:			
Attempted CSE	21·1	36·6	68·4
Obtained Grade 5 or better in:			
1 or more subjects	20·9	36·3	66·9
3 or more subjects	15·3	27·9	50·0
5 or more subjects	9·4	19·6	33·2
Obtained Grade 1 in:			
1 or more subjects	7·5	15·2	24·7
3 or more subjects	1·1	3·0	4·7
5 or more subjects	0·2	0·7	1·1

1. Provisional.
2. From 1974/75, 'O' level passes at grades A–C only.
3. The Certificate of Secondary Education was introduced in 1965.

Table 88

**Destination and achievements
of school leavers
England and Wales**

percentage

	1966/67	1971/72	1975/76[1]
Males			
Universities	7·8	7·3	7·5
Colleges of education[2]	1·5	1·4	0·5
Polytechnics	—	2·3	2·4
Other full-time further education	8·6	8·3	8·5
Employment	82·0	80·7	81·1
Thousands of leavers (=100%)	306·0	332·3	363·9
Leavers with:			
At least 2 'A' levels	14·0	13·9	14·0
At least 5 'O' levels or 1 or more			
'A' level passes[3]	23·8	24·7	22·3
No G C E or C S E passes	—	42·8	18·9
Females			
Universities	3·8	4·2	4·5
Colleges of education[2]	5·2	5·1	2·2
Polytechnics	—	1·3	1·6
Other full-time further education	12·2	13·7	17·1
Employment	78·9	75·7	74·6
Thousands of leavers (=100%)	288·9	312·5	343·6
Leavers with:			
At least 2 'A' levels	9·4	11·4	11·5
At least 5 'O' levels or 1 or more			
'A' level passes[3]	22·0	24·9	22·2
No G C E or C S E passes	—	44·0	17·0

1. Provisional.
2. Including teacher training courses at polytechnics and other establishments.
3. Including 'O' level passes on 'A' level papers and Grade 1 results in the CSE examination. From 1974/75, 'O' level passes at grades A–C only.

Table 89
Training of teachers
United Kingdom

	At October		number
	1965	1970	1975
Total students in initial training courses	87,257	130,719	119,160
Men			
Courses for graduates, one-year	2,696[1]	4,375[1]	6,200[2]
Courses for non-graduates:			
One-year	1,441	1,701	2,243
Two-year	857	879	481
Three-year and four-year	19,944	30,099	24,999
Women			
Courses for graduates, one-year	2,739	5,216	6,702[3]
Courses for non-graduates:			
One-year	1,040	1,775	2,098
Two-year	1,400	1,882	891
Three-year and four-year	57,107	84,792	75,546

1. Includes 18 students on a two-year course in 1970.
2. Includes 13 students on a two-year course in 1975.
3. Includes 2 students on a two-year course in 1975.

Table 90

Teachers' qualifications
England and Wales

percentage

	1964/65	1969/70	1974/75[1]
Public sector schools			
Men			
Qualified graduates			
Trained	22·3	21·9	27·9
Untrained	8·5	8·3	8·2
Qualified non-graduates	68·0	69·8	63·9
Non-qualified	1·2	··	··
Thousands of teachers (=100%)	122	137	168
Women			
Qualified graduates			
Trained	9·4	9·7	14·3
Untrained	3·7	3·9	3·6
Qualified non-graduates	83·5	86·4	82·1
Non-qualified	3·4	··	··
Thousands of teachers (=100%)	162	191	250

1. Provisional.

Table 91

Nursery education[1]
United Kingdom

At January | | percentage

	1966	1971	1976
Full-time and part-time pupils as a percentage of all children aged 2–4:			
Public sector	9·0	12·5	21·1
Assisted and independent schools	1·2	1·2	1·3
Total	10·2	13·7	22·5
Total pupils (thousands)	288·1	382·0	546·9

1. Excluding special schools.

Table 92

**Further education:
establishments maintained or
assisted by local authorities or
receiving direct grants
United Kingdom**

	1965	1970	1975[1]
England and Wales (November)			
Number of establishments	8,202	7,174	7,835
Polytechnics	—	26	30
National Colleges	7		
Regional Colleges	25		
Art establishments	153	} 646	545
Agricultural establishments	45		
Other major establishments	517		
Evening institutes	7,455	6,502	7,260
Number of students (thousands)			
Full-time	169·8	237·8	351·2
Sandwich	17·2	36·5	46·7
Part-time day	679·8	748·7	743·3
Evening – major establishments	795·9	736·4	801·6
– evening institutes	1,252·9	1,421·8	1,981·7
Scotland (Session, end year)			
Number of establishments[2]	1,152	1,164	211
Central institutions	14	13	14
Further education centres			
day	92	82	74
evening	1,046	1,069	123
Number of students (thousands)[2]			
Full-time	16·1	24·7	35·0
Part-time	311·4	332·4	129·3
Northern Ireland (Summer term)			
Polytechnics	—	—	1
Number of institutions of further			
education	32	31	28
Number of students (thousands)			
Grant aided institutions	51·4	62·4	61·1
Ulster college			
(The NI polytechnic)	—	—	4·8

1. Provisional figures for England and Wales.
2. Non-vocational included for earlier sessions; excluded in 1975.

Table 93
**Universities
United Kingdom**

thousands

	1966/67	1971/72	1975/76
Full-time students enrolled			
Men	138·6	170·2	178·1
Women	51·3	72·3	90·6
Students taking courses			
Full-time undergraduate			
Men	112·4	135·3	140·8
Women	44·4	62·0	77·3
Full-time postgraduate			
Men	25·8	35·0	37·3
Women	6·7	10·3	13·4
Part-time undergraduate			
Men	2·9	2·3	2·0
Women	1·4	1·4	1·8
Part-time postgraduate			
Men	11·3	16·1	17·3
Women	1·8	3·7	5·2
Home residence of full-time students			
United Kingdom	172·7	222·7	237·2
Overseas	17·1	19·9	31·5
Degrees and diplomas obtained by full-time students			
First degrees (honours)	27·4	41·4	44·7
First degrees (ordinary)	9·8	10·3	11·0
Higher degrees	8·0	11·3	16·1
Diplomas	12·9	10·9	13·7
Full-time teaching staff[1]			
Professors	2·7	3·5	4·0
Readers and Senior lecturers	4·5	6·0	7·6
Lecturers	12·7		
Assistant lecturers and demonstrators	3·1	19·2	19·7
Others	1·0	0·9	0·9

1. Wholly financed from general university funds.

Table 94

University courses
United Kingdom

percentage

	1971/72	1975/76
Courses taken by full-time undergraduates		
Education	0·5	1·0
Medicine, dentistry and health	11·2	11·9
Engineering and technology	15·9	13·8
Agriculture, forestry and veterinary science	1·8	1·9
Science	24·9	23·0
Social, administrative and business studies	21·2	23·5
Architecture and other professional and vocational subjects	1·7	1·8
Language, literature and area studies	12·8	12·8
Arts other than languages	10·1	10·3
Thousands of undergraduates (=100%)	197·3	218·1
Courses taken by full-time postgraduates		
Education	17·9	17·8
Medicine, dentistry and health	5·3	5·8
Engineering and technology	14·4	13·7
Agriculture, forestry and veterinary science	2·3	2·2
Science	25·1	23·9
Social, administrative and business studies	19·2	20·8
Architecture and other professional and vocational subjects	2·7	3·5
Language, literature and area studies	6·9	6·6
Arts other than languages	6·2	5·5
Thousands of postgraduates (=100%)	45·3	50·6

Table 95

**Destination of
graduates[1]
United Kingdom**

	1966/67 Total	1971/72 Total	1975/76		
			Men	Women	Total
Entering employment					
First degrees	14,775	17,229	13,377	5,905	19,282
Higher degrees	2,598	4,253	3,377	810	4,187
Total	17,373	21,482	16,754	6,715	23,469
Proceeding to further study or training					
First degrees	15,190	19,737	9,982	7,535	17,517
Higher degrees	1,332	1,938	1,809	350	2,159
Total	16,522	21,675	11,791	7,885	19,676

1. Figures do not include graduates in medicine, dentistry or veterinary science.

Education

Percentage of students studying : 1975/76

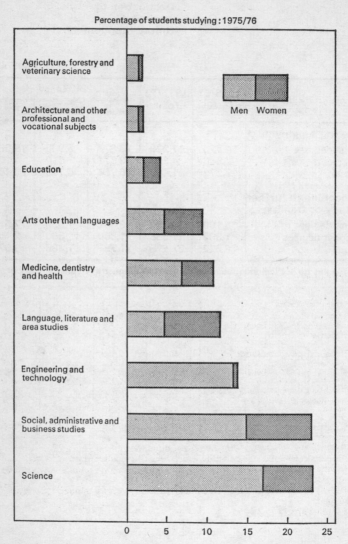

Chart 15: University full-time students: subject groups of study United Kingdom

Table 96

Employment on scientific research in 1972–73 United Kingdom

thousands

	Scientists and engineers	Tech- nicians[1]	Others[2]	Total
Industry[3,4]				
Mining and quarrying	0·3	0·4	0·2	0·9
Food, drink and tobacco	1·7	2·9	2·0	6·6
Chemical and allied products	10·0	13·4	8·2	31·6
Iron and steel	1·5	1·1	0·9	3·5
Non-ferrous metals	0·6	0·6	0·4	1·6
Mechanical engineering	4·4	4·6	4·1	13·1
Scientific instruments and systems	1·6	2·0	1·5	5·1
Electrical engineering	20·1	18·2	13·8	52·1
Ships and marine engines	0·5	0·3	0·5	1·3
Motor vehicles	3·1	4·1	6·2	13·4
Aerospace	10·4	10·3	14·7	35·4
Other manufactures	4·8	5·0	4·0	13·8
Construction	0·2	0·2	0·3	0·7
Utilities and services	1·6	1·0	0·8	3·4
Total industry	60·8	64·1	57·6	182·5
Central government[4]				
Defence	6·5	6·6	22·9	36·0
Industry, trade and employment	4·3	3·9	11·1	19·3
of which: Aerospace[5]	(0·6)	(0·6)	(2·5)	(3·7)
Atomic energy	(3·0)	(2·3)	(7·5)	(12·8)
Agriculture, fisheries and forestry	0·8	0·9	1·5	3·2
Environmental services	0·8	0·9	1·3	3·0
Agricultural Research Council	0·5	0·7	0·8	2·0
Medical Research Council	1·0	1·7	1·4	4·1
Natural Environment Research Council	0·9	0·2	1·4	2·5
Science Research Council	0·5	0·5	1·9	2·9
Other	0·6	0·7	1·5	2·8
Total central government	15·9	16·1	43·8	75·8

1. Technicians, laboratory assistants and draughtsmen
2. Administrative and clerical staff and others (including industrial staff).
3. Private industry, research associations and public corporations, analysed by product group.
4. Full-time equivalents at 31 December (Industry) and 1 January (Central government).
5. 1 April 1973.

Table 97

Expenditure on scientific research and development United Kingdom

£ million

	Cost of work done		Source of funds	
	1969/70	1972/73	1969/70	1972/73
Government	262·7	336·7	529·3[1]	640·1[1]
of which : Defence	(104·8)	(133·0)	(220·6)	(327·3)
Research Councils	(46·9)	(64·2)	(72·5)	(106·1)
Other civil	(111·0)	(139·5)	(236·2)[2]	(206·7)[2]
Universities and further education establishments	80·4	115·6	10·0	13·2
Research associations	16·4	18·8	0·6	0·4
Private industry	619·0	739·2	396·8	491·4
Public corporations	44·9	69·2	51·7	76·1
Other	22·0	30·6	57·0	88·9
Total	1,045·4	1,310·1	1,045·4	1,310·1

1. As reported by performing sectors.
2. Includes net difference between total in (1) and total as returned by government.

Table 98

Central government expenditure on natural and social sciences, and engineering

£ million

	1972/73	1973/74	1974/75	1975/76
EEC objectives classification				
Exploration and exploitation of the earth and atmosphere	4·1	4·0	6·4	8·1
Planning of the human environment	13·1	16·1	20·8	29·5
Protection and improvement of human health	16·0	23·8	27·7	38·3
Agricultural productivity and technology	20·6	30·6	42·2	53·0
Production, distribution and rational use of energy	178·8	56·6	68·6	87·0
Industrial productivity and technology		125·9	161·2	147·7
Social and sociological problems	5·6	5·9	8·0	11·4
Exploration and exploitation of space	11·5	19·8	22·5	27·0
Defence	351·8	406·6	503·1	553·5
General promotion of knowledge	175·1	182·0	214·9	237·1
Total	776·6	871·3	1,075·4	1,192·6

1. Estimated.

Table 99

**Economic activity
Population Census
United Kingdom**

thousands

	1951[2]	1961	1971
Population aged 15 and over[1]	38,922	40,582	42,007
– as percentage of population, all ages	77·5	77·0	75·7
Economically active			
Males			
Total	16,070	16,648	16,296
In employment			
Self-employed and employers	1,421	1,464	1,540
Employees	14,279	14,658	13,862
Out of employment[3]			
Sick	} 370	525	894
Other			
Females			
Total	7,144	7,969	9,338
In employment			
Self-employed and employers	317	341	381
Employees	6,681	7,421	8,511
Out of employment[3]			
Sick	} 145	207	446
Other			
Economically inactive			
Males			
Total	2,278	2,646	3,716
Retired	1,554	1,855	2,362
Students in educational establishments	} 724	556	964
Others		234	389
Females			
Total	13,431	13,320	12,658
Retired	321	657	3,055
Students in educational establishments	} 13,109	470	843
Others		12,192	8,760

1. The population aged 15 and over and the percentage are calculated using the enumerated population. For the economically active and the economically inactive the following figures were used: 1951 the enumerated population; 1961 the 10 per cent sample taking no account of the bias; 1971 the 10 per cent sample.

2. In 1951 the figures for Northern Ireland are for those aged 14 and over.

3. The breakdown of 'Out of employment' into 'Sick' and 'Other' is not available for Northern Ireland.

Table 100
**Distribution of total working population[1]
United Kingdom**

At mid-June   thousands

	1966	1971	1973	1975	1976
Total working population	25,632	25,123	25,545	25,834	26,084
Males	16,783	16,219	16,172	16,112	16,225
Females	8,851	8,904	9,373	9,722	9,857
Unemployed	281	724	575	866	1,332
Males	221	618	483	707	1,009
Females	61	106	92	159	322
Employed labour force	25,351	24,399	24,970	24,968	24,752
Males	16,562	15,601	15,689	15,405	15,216
Females	8,790	8,798	9,281	9,563	9,535
HM Forces and Women's Services	417	368	361	336	336
Males	402	353	346	322	321
Females	15	15	15	15	15
Employers and self-employed persons	1,681	1,909	1,947	1,925	1,925
Males	1,317	1,534	1,572	1,551	1,551
Females	365	375	375	374	374
Total employees in employment	23,253	22,122	22,662	22,707	22,491
Males	14,843	13,714	13,771	13,532	13,344
Females	8,410	8,408	8,891	9,174	9,146

1. From 1971, the employees in employment estimates are based on an annual census of employment taken in June each year which excludes private domestic servants and civil servants temporarily stationed outside the United Kingdom. For the years before 1971, estimates of employees in employment are taken from the continuous employment series which was published in the October 1975 issue of the *Department of Employment Gazette*. This continuous series allowed for the discontinuities which were present in the previously published series.

Table 101

**Labour force:[1] projections
and age distribution
Great Britain**

	Actual		Projected	
	1971[2]	1976[3]	1981[3]	1986[3]
Economically active (thousands)				
Total	25,018	25,868	26,734	27,781
Males	15,933	15,914	16,164	16,603
Females	9,085	9,954	10,570	11,178
of whom – married	5,799	6,731	7,129	7,705
others	3,286	3,223	3,441	3,473
Percentage distribution of economically active by age and sex				
Males:				
aged 16–19	4·3	4·2	4·4	4·0
20–24	7·6	6·6	7·0	7·4
25–44	25·9	26·5	26·7	27·3
45–64	23·8	22·4	20·9	19·8
65 and over	2·1	1·8	1·5	1·3
Total aged 16 and over	63·7	61·5	60·5	59·8
Females – married:				
aged 16–19	0·3	0·3	0·3	0·3
20–24	2·2	2·2	2·2	2·4
25–44	10·5	12·7	13·3	14·2
45–59	8·7	9·4	9·3	9·2
60 and over	1·5	1·4	1·5	1·6
Total aged 16 and over	23·2	26·0	26·7	27·7
Females – other:				
aged 16–19	3·4	3·3	3·4	3·1
20–24	2·7	2·4	2·8	2·9
25–44	2·6	2·9	3·1	3·3
45–59	3·0	2·7	2·4	2·1
60 and over	1·5	1·2	1·1	1·1
Total aged 16 and over	13·1	12·5	12·9	12·5

1. Excluding students.
2. Estimates are based on the 1971 Census of Population (100 per cent) count. They have been adjusted to be consistent with data for later years by (i) excluding those aged 15, and (ii) including UK forces stationed abroad and excluding foreign forces stationed in the UK.
3. Data relate to mid-year and are provisional.

Table 102

**Employees by industry group
United Kingdom**

	At June	thousands
	1975	1976[1]
Total employees in employment	22,707	22,491
Agriculture, forestry, fishing	401·0	392·9
Mining and quarrying	352·2	344·4
Manufacturing	7,488·1	7,290·1
Food, drink and tobacco	725·7	718·3
Coal and petroleum products	39·5	38·4
Chemicals and allied industries	430·4	425·8
Metal manufacture	501·1	473·7
Mechanical engineering	959·8	930·3
Instrument engineering	155·7	148·0
Electrical engineering	780·9	744·8
Shipbuilding and marine engineering	184·2	181·7
Vehicles	756·3	735·4
Metal goods not elsewhere specified	545·6	529·6
Textiles	529·4	521·8
Leather, leather goods and fur	41·8	42·2
Clothing and footwear	402·4	395·3
Bricks, pottery, glass, cement, etc.	275·8	267·0
Timber, furniture, etc.	263·9	264·3
Paper, printing and publishing	565·2	542·2
Other manufacturing industries	330·4	331·2
Construction	1,312·8	1,271·2
Gas, electricity and water	353·3	343·7
Transport and communication	1,518·0	1,484·7
Distributive trades	2,762·7	2,708·2
Insurance, banking, finance and business services	1,103·0	1,109·7
Professional and scientific services	3,555·8	3,621·3
Hotels, restaurants, public houses, clubs, catering contractors	825·8	825·7
Miscellaneous services (excluding hotels, restaurants, etc.)	1,376·3	1,398·5
National government service	649·9	670·4
Local government service	1,004·6	1,030·5

1. Provisional.

Table 103

Civil service staff[1]
United Kingdom
Analysis by ministerial responsibility[2]

	At 1 April		thousands
	1971	1975[3]	1977[3]
Total civil and defence departments	700·1	701·4	745·6
Total civil departments:	418·2	434·8	486·9
Agriculture, Fisheries and Food	15·9	15·8	15·5
Chancellor of the Exchequer's Departments	106·5	119·8	129·3
Customs and Excise	17·9	28·4	29·3
Inland Revenue	69·8	74·2	83·9
Department for National Savings	15·0	13·3	12·2
Treasury and others	3·8	3·9	3·9
Education and Science	7·4	4·0	4·0
Employment	32·3	19·2	52·5
Energy	·	1·3	1·3
Environment	76·0	75·2	61·5
Foreign and Commonwealth	13·1	12·6	12·4
Home	26·0	30·7	32·6
Industry	·	10·4	9·7
Prices and Consumer Protection	·	0·4	0·4
Social services	74·1	91·5	98·3
Trade	27·7	9·2	9·7
Transport	·	·	13·6
Other civil departments	39·1	44·7	46·1
Ministry of Defence	281·9	266·6	258·7

1. The figures include established and unestablished non-industrial and industrial staff but exclude casual or seasonal staff and employees of the Northern Ireland Government. Two part-time employees are counted as one whole-time employee.

2. The figures for 1971 have been adjusted to show staff in current Ministerial areas so that the figures in all columns are on a comparable basis.

3. For 1975 and 1977 the figures exclude certain staff not employed by government departments but deemed to be civil servants for superannuation purposes, the staff of the Parliamentary Commissioner for Administration and the Exchequer and Audit Department, and certain judicial officers.

Table 104
**Unemployment
United Kingdom**

Monthly averages

	1970	1972	1974[1]	1976[1]
Total unemployed (thousands)	618·0	885·5	631·0	1,358·8
Males	522·9	735·6	523·8	1,025·1
Females	95·1	149·9	107·2	332·5
As a percentage of the number of employees – total	2·6	3·9	2·7	5·8
Males	3·6	5·1	3·7	7·3
Females	1·1	1·7	1·2	3·6

1. The 1974 total, male and female averages and the total average for 1976 are for eleven months. The male and female averages for 1976 are for ten months.

Table 105
**Male unemployment rates by region
United Kingdom**

Monthly averages

	1970	1972	1974[1]	1976[1]
Unemployed males as a percentage of all male employees				
United Kingdom	3·6	5·1	3·6	7·3
Great Britain	3·4	5·0	3·6	7·1
North[2]	6·2	8·1	6·1	9·0
Yorkshire and Humberside[2]	3·9	5·6	3·7	6·9
East Midlands[2]	3·0	4·1	3·0	6·0
East Anglia	2·9	3·9	2·7	6·2
South East[2]	2·3	3·0	2·2	5·5
South West[2]	3·7	4·5	3·6	8·2
West Midlands	2·6	4·7	2·8	7·2
North West[2]	3·8	6·6	4·9	9·0
Wales	4·8	6·0	4·9	9·0
Scotland	5·5	8·3	5·4	8·6
Northern Ireland	8·5	9·5	7·0	11·7

1. The figures for 1974 are the averages of eleven months, and for 1976 the averages of ten months.
2. The boundaries of the region were revised in April 1974. The averages for 1974 are for the revised region, which differs slightly from the old area.

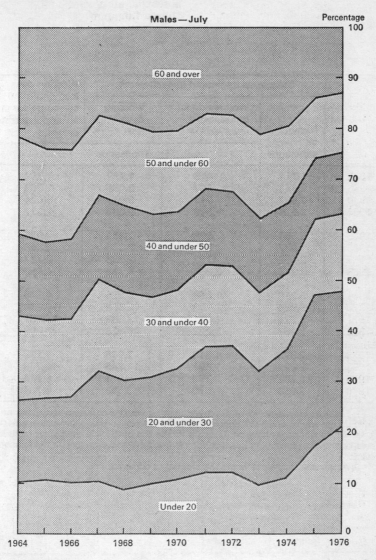

Males — July

Percentage

60 and over

50 and under 60

40 and under 50

30 and under 40

20 and under 30

Under 20

1964 1966 1968 1970 1972 1974 1976

**Chart 16: Males unemployed
by age
Great Britain**

Table 106

Industrial stoppages[1]
United Kingdom

	Stoppages beginning in each year[2]			Working days lost within the calendar year in all stoppages in progress
	Number of stoppages	Workers directly or indirectly involved[3]	Working days lost	
		Thousands		
1952	1,714	415	1,797	1,792
1956	2,648	507	2,051	2,083
1960	2,832	817	3,049	3,024
1964	2,524	873	2,030	2,277
1965	2,354	868	2,932	2,925
1966	1,937	531	2,395	2,398
1967	2,116	732	2,783	2,787
1968	2,378	2,256	4,719	4,690
1969	3,116	1,656	6,925	6,846
1970	3,906	1,793	10,908	10,980
1971	2,228	1,171	13,589	13,551
1972	2,497	1,722	23,923	23,909
1973	2,873	1,513	7,145	7,197
1974	2,922	1,601	14,845	14,740
1975	2,282	789	5,914	6,012
1976	2,016	670	3,509	3,284

1. Excludes stoppages involving fewer than 10 workers or lasting less than one day except any in which the aggregate number of working days lost exceeded 100.
2. Where stoppages have continued after the end of the year the figures include workers (if any) becoming involved for the first time, and days lost, in the following year.
3. At the establishments where the stoppages occurred.

Table 107
Trade unions[1]

At end of year

	1966	1971	1975
Number of trade unions	622	523	488
Analysis by number of members:			
Under 100 members	127	100	73
100–499	147	128	133
500–999	66	60	52
1,000–2,499	89	65	68
2,500–4,999	66	53	44
5,000–9,999	30	33	30
10,000–14,999	22	11	11
15,000–24,999	18	19	17
25,000–49,999	19	16	20
50,000–99,999	20	15	15
100,000–249,999	9	12	14
Over 250,000	9	11	11
Membership (thousands)			
Total	10,261	11,128	11,950
Males[2]	8,006	8,378	8,508
Females[2]	2,256	2,750	3,442

1. All organizations of employees with head offices in the United Kingdom which are known to include among their functions that of negotiating with employers with the object of regulating the conditions of employment of their members.
2. The subdivision of the total membership into males and females is partly estimated.

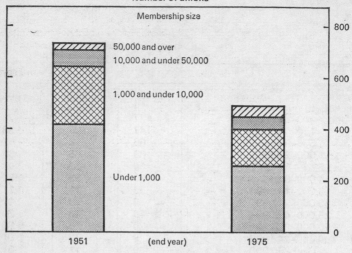

Number of unions

Membership size

50,000 and over

10,000 and under 50,000

1,000 and under 10,000

Under 1,000

1951 (end year) 1975

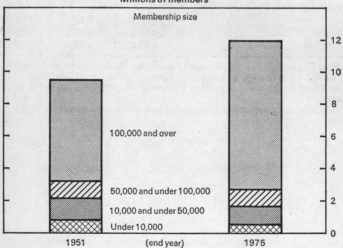

Millions of members

Membership size

100,000 and over

50,000 and under 100,000

10,000 and under 50,000

Under 10,000

1951 (end year) 1975

Chart 17: Trade unions:
membership
United Kingdom

Table 108

Number of full-time adults by range of earnings, April 1976 Great Britain

Estimates of total number in employment with gross weekly earnings below specified amounts[1]

millions

	Men aged 21 and over			Women aged 18 and over		
	Total	Manual	Non-manual	Total	Manual	Non-manual
Gross weekly earnings[2]						
Under £25	—	—	—	0·2	0·1	0·1
£27	0·1	—	—	0·4	0·2	0·2
£30	0·1	—	—	0·7	0·3	0·4
£32	0·1	0·1	0·1	0·9	0·3	0·6
£35	0·2	0·1	0·1	1·3	0·5	0·8
£37	0·3	0·2	0·1	1·6	0·6	1·0
£40	0·5	0.3	0·2	2·0	0·7	1·3
£45	1·1	0·7	0·4	2·7	0·9	1·7
£50	1·9	1·3	0·6	3·2	1·1	2·1
£55	2·9	2·0	0·9	3·6	1·2	2·4
£60	3·9	2·7	1·2	3·9	1·3	2·6
£65	4·9	3·4	1·5	4·1	1·3	2·8
£70	5·9	4·0	1·8	4·2	1·3	2·9
£75	6·7	4·5	2·1	4·3	1·3	3·0
£80	7·3	4·9	2·4	4·4	1·3	3·1
£85	7·9	5·2	2·7	4·5	1·3	3·2
£90	8·3	5·5	2·9	4·5	1·3	3·2
£100	8·9	5·7	3·2	4·6	1·3	3·3
£120	9·6	6·0	3·7	4·7	1·3	3·3
£150	10·0	6·0	4·0	4·7	1·3	3·4
£200	10·1	6·1	4·1	4·7	1·3	3·4
£250	10·2	6·1	4·1	4·7	1·3	3·4
Number of full-time adults whose pay was not affected by absence	10·2	6·1	4·1	4·7	1·3	3·4
Number of full-time adults in employment	11·3	7·0	4·3	5·2	1·6	3·6

1. Excluding those whose pay was affected by absence in the pay-period.
2. The total earnings of the employee for the survey pay-period, as reported by the employer, before any statutory or other deductions.

Table 109

Number of earners by regions and range of earnings, April 1976 Great Britain

Adults paid for a full week

	Number in sample	Percentage with weekly earnings less than:				
		£35	£40	£50	£70	£100
Men aged 21 and over						
Great Britain	85,160	2·1	5·2	18·4	57·5	87·7
North	4,897	1·7	4·4	16·2	55·8	89·2
Yorkshire and Humberside	7,755	2·2	5·9	20·3	61·3	90·2
East Midlands	5,881	2·0	5·2	20·6	63·8	91·9
East Anglia	2,716	2·4	6·8	26·1	66·5	90·9
South East	27,355	2·0	4·5	15·3	51·1	82·9
Greater London	13,826	1·9	3·8	12·5	44·7	78·2
Remainder of South East	13,529	2·2	5·1	18·2	57·6	87·8
South West	5,991	3·2	7·0	24·7	65·1	90·2
West Midlands	8,205	1·8	4·9	17·2	60·4	91·6
North West	10,102	2·2	5·3	18·6	59·6	89·1
Wales	4,087	2·0	5·5	19·1	59·4	89·9
Scotland	8,171	2·5	5·7	19·8	57·0	87·2
Women aged 18 and over						
Great Britain	35,999	27·7	43·2	68·9	89·8	98·2
North	2,059	29·6	46·3	72·9	90·2	98·2
Yorkshire and Humberside	2,980	32·9	51·5	76·3	92·9	98·8
East Midlands	2,286	33·8	51·0	77·2	92·8	99·0
East Anglia	974	34·7	50·9	76·2	97·1	98·7
South East	12,045	20·3	33·3	58·9	86·6	97·5
Greater London	6,547	13·8	23·9	49·8	83·9	96·8
Remainder of South East	5,498	28·2	44·6	69·7	89·9	98·2
South West	2,284	32·7	49·0	71·9	90·5	98·8
West Midlands	3,315	29·8	46·4	73·4	91·0	98·4
North West	4,467	31·4	48·0	73·9	91·4	98·4
Wales	1,591	28·6	43·6	71·3	89·9	98·4
Scotland	3,998	30·9	47·1	72·8	91·8	98·3

1. Excluding those whose pay was affected by absence.

Table 110

Average weekly earnings and hours of full-time manual workers
United Kingdom

October

	Males aged 21 and over	Females aged 18 and over
Average weekly earnings[1] (£)		
1962	15·86	8·04
1963	16·75	8·41
1964	18·11	8·95
1965	19·59	9·60
1966	20·30	10·07
1967	21·38	10·56
1968	23·00	11·30
1969	24·83	12·11
1970	28·05	13·99
1971	30·93	15·80
1972	35·82	18·30
1973	40·92	21·16
1974	48·63	27·01
1975	59·58	34·19
1976	66·97	40·61
Average weekly hours worked		
1962	47·0	39·4
1963	47·6	39·7
1964	47·7	39·4
1965	47·0	38·7
1966	46·0	38·1
1967	46·2	38·2
1968	46·4	38·3
1969	46·5	38·1
1970	45·7	37·9
1971	44·7	37·7
1972	45·0	37·9
1973	45·6	37·7
1974	45·1	37·4
1975	43·6	37·0
1976	44·0	37·4

1. Exclusive of National Insurance contributions and taxes.

Table 111

**Index numbers of basic wage
rates and normal weekly hours
of manual workers
United Kingdom**

31 July 1972 = 100

	Basic weekly wage	Basic hourly wage	Normal weekly hours
All industries and services			
1956	42·0	37·8	111·1
1957	44·1	39·8	111·0
1958	45·7	41·2	110·8
1959	46·9	42·3	110·7
1960	48·1	44·2	108·9
1961	50·1	47·0	106·6
1962	51·9	49·1	105·7
1963	53·8	51·0	105·6
1964	56·4	53·6	105·1
1965	58·8	57·0	103·2
1966	61·5	60·8	101·2
1967	63·8	63·2	101·0
1968	68·1	67·6	100·8
1969	71·7	71·2	100·7
1970	78·8	78·5	100·4
1971	89·0	88·9	100·1
1972	101·3	101·4	99·9
1973	115·2	115·6	99·6
1974	138·0	138·7	99·5
1975	178·7	179·8	99·4
1976	213·2	214·5	99·4

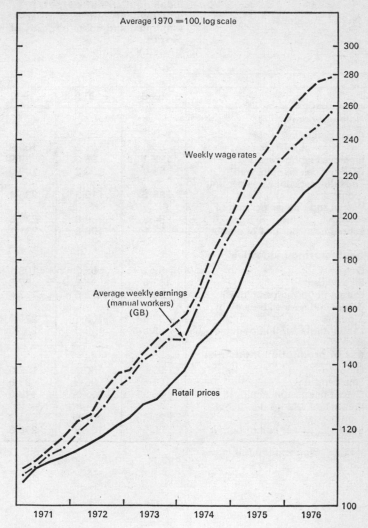

Average 1970 = 100, log scale

Weekly wage rates

Average weekly earnings
(manual workers)
(GB)

Retail prices

**Chart 18: Earnings, wage
rates and retail prices
United Kingdom**

Table 112

Index numbers of output, employment, output per person employed and costs per unit of output
United Kingdom
1970 = 100

	1966	1971	1976
Whole economy			
Gross domestic product (income at 1970 prices)	90·9	101·5	108·9
Employed labour force[1]	102·2	98·3	99·9
GDP per person employed[1]	89·0	103·3	109·0
Total domestic incomes per unit of output	84·1	110·3	235·4
Wages and salaries per unit of output	84·8	108·8	226·5
Labour costs per unit of output	83·1	108·8	231·1
Manufacturing industries			
Output	89·2	99·2	103·1
Employment	102·6	96·8	87·8
Output per person employed	86·9	102·5	117·4
Wages and salaries per unit of output	82·9	109·1	220·9
Labour costs per unit of output	83·5	109·6	232·0
Index of production industries			
Output	90·6	100·1	102·0
Employment	105·6	96·9	89·9
Output per person employed	85·8	103·3	113·5
Wages and salaries per unit of output	85·9	107·5	231·3
Labour costs per unit of output	85·5	107·8	240·8

1. Civil employment and HM Forces.

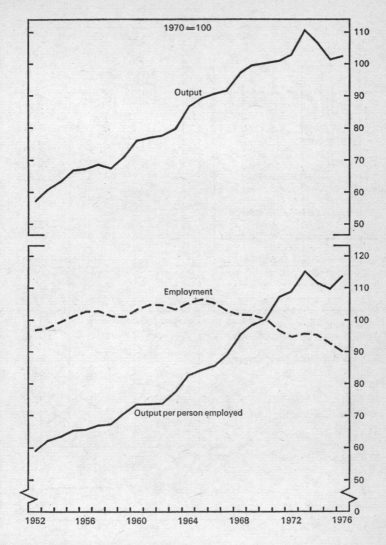

1970 = 100

Output

Employment

Output per person employed

1952   1956   1960   1964   1968   1972   1976

**Chart 19: Index of production
industries: output, employment,
output per person employed
United Kingdom**

X Leisure

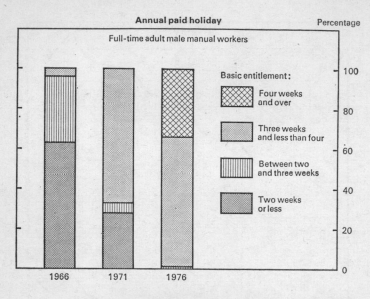

Annual paid holiday   Percentage

Full-time adult male manual workers

Basic entitlement:

Four weeks and over

Three weeks and less than four

Between two and three weeks

Two weeks or less

1966   1971   1976

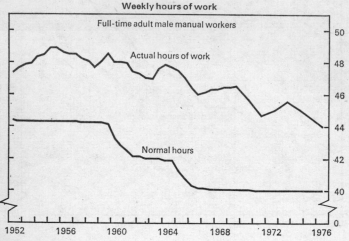

Weekly hours of work

Full-time adult male manual workers

Actual hours of work

Normal hours

1952   1956   1960   1964   1968   1972   1976

*Chart 20: Annual paid
holiday and weekly hours
of work
United Kingdom*

Table 113

**Leisure activities:
by social class, 1970**

percentage

	Professional and managerial	Clerical	Skilled	Semi-skilled and unskilled	All
Proportion in each class doing selected activity at least monthly in previous year:					
Home-based activities					
Watching television	95	99	98	95	97
Gardening	70	62	66	50	64
Playing with children	59	63	66	59	62
Home decorations/ repairs	52	55	56	45	53
Car cleaning	55	44	51	35	48
Playing an instrument	10	8	5	4	7
Total number of home-based activities engaged in at least monthly	*5·7*	*5·9*	*5·2*	*4·2*	*5·3*
Sporting activities					
Swimming	34	25	20	8	22
Fishing	9	3	9	5	8
Table tennis	10	10	4	2	6
Sailing	6	—	1	—	2
Total number of sporting activities engaged in at least monthly					
Active sports	*1·1*	*0·8*	*0·6*	*0·3*	*0·7*
Spectator sports	*0·4*	*0·3*	*0·5*	*0·3*	*0·4*
Other leisure activities					
Going for a drive	62	51	62	49	58
Going to a pub	51	42	54	58	52
Going for a walk	56	63	41	36	47
Going out for a meal	48	31	25	23	32
Attending church	22	20	12	7	15
Total number of activities engaged in at least monthly	*3·5*	*3·3*	*2·8*	*2·5*	*3·0*

Table 114

**Leisure activities by sex, 1973
Great Britain**

percentage

	Persons engaging in activity frequently[1]			Persons engaging in activity rarely[2]		
	Men	Women		Men	Women	
		In full-time employment	Other		In full-time employment	Other
Activities at home:						
Watching television	92	87	92	3	9	5
Reading papers	84	63	80	4	9	8
Relaxing	73	62	73	17	27	19
Listening to music	57	66	69	13	13	15
Reading books	37	39	41	39	38	43
Activities not at home:						
Visiting friends, family	69	75	73	11	11	9
Going to pub, etc.	62	62	31	29	29	54
Going out for a meal	35	36	21	26	19	35
Clubs, societies	25	19	18	56	75	74
Taking part in sport	32	13	7	63	81	91
Watching sport	31	8	5	52	77	80
Cinema, theatre, etc.	18	24	9	51	37	54
Going to bingo	7	13	13	90	86	84

1. Respondents engaging in activities at home for an hour a day or more; for activities outside the home, 'frequently' means two or three times a month or more.
2. Respondents engaging in activities at home for less than an hour a month; for activities outside home, 'rarely' means less than once a year.

Leisure

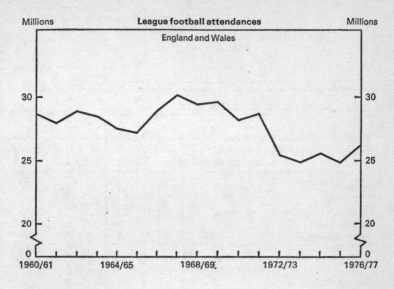

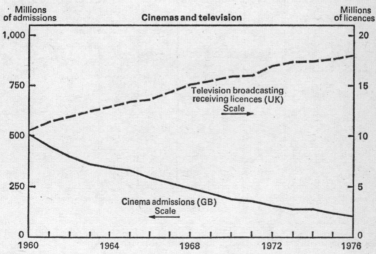

Chart 21: Leisure activities

Table 115

Cinema admissions and television licences[1]

	1966	1971	1976
Cinema			
Number of cinemas reporting	1,847	1,482	1,525
Number of admissions (millions)	288·8	176·0	103·9
Total gross box office takings (£ million)	59·4	60·3	75·8
Average price of admission (p)	20·6	34·3	73·0
Television			
Licences current at 31 December (thousands)			
Monochrome	13,919	15,263	8,426
Colour	—	1,305	9,569

1. Figures on cinemas are for Great Britain; figures on television licences are for the United Kingdom.

Table 116

Television viewing
United Kingdom

	February			August		
	1967	1971	1976	1967	1971	1976
Average weekly hours viewed by:						
Males aged 5–14	19·1	21·5	} 22·0	15·9	19·7	} 19·0
Females aged 5–14	17·6	19·9		14·7	17·8	
Males aged 15 and over	14·5	16·9	..	11·9	13·4	..
Females aged 15 and over	16·9	19·6	..	13·8	15·1	..
Social class A[1]	12·8	14·0	16·6	10·4	12·7	11·3
Social class B[2]	14·3	16·8	17·7	12·0	13·1	12·5
Social class C[3]	16·6	19·1	20·3	13·4	15·0	14·6
Overall average weekly hours viewed by persons aged 5 and over	16·2	18·6	19·9	13·4	15·0	14·7

Social class: BBC definition

1. Members of families in which the chief wage earner is a doctor, professor, clergyman, lawyer, architect; owner, director, senior executive of a large commercial or industrial organization; senior civil servant; or high ranking industrial technician such as scientist or consulting engineer. This group covers about five per cent of the population.

2. Members of families in which the chief wage earner is a bank clerk, more senior office worker, teacher, small employer; manager or shopkeeper of larger shops; supervisor in a factory; professional worker not coming into class A. Class B covers about twenty-five per cent of the population.

3. The remaining seventy per cent of the population.

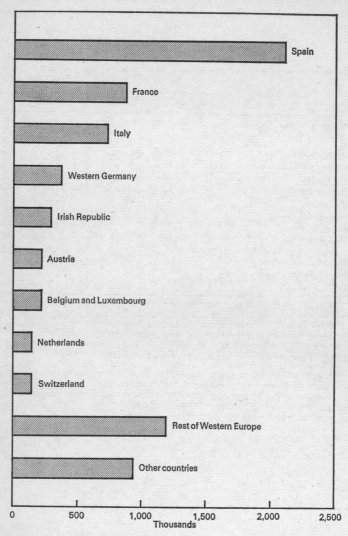

Chart 22: Holidays taken abroad by United Kingdom residents in 1976

Table 117
Holidays

percentage

	1966	1971	1976[1]
Holiday[2] visits abroad by GB residents			
Austria	7	7	3
Belgium/Luxembourg	4	3	3
France	14	10	12
Irish Republic	9	6	4
Italy	17	8	10
Netherlands	3	3	2
Spain/Majorca	22	34	29
Switzerland	7	4	2
Western Germany	7	6	5
Rest of Europe	5	10	18
Other countries[3]	5	9	12
Total visits (thousands = 100%)[3]	5,500	7,250	7,250
Holidays[4] taken in Great Britain by residents of Great Britain (millions)	31	34	38

1. Provisional.
2. Holiday as defined by the respondent in the International Passenger Survey.
3. Includes holidays on cruise ships not assigned to particular areas.
4. Defined in the British National Travel Survey as trips of four or more nights away from home, considered to be holidays by the travellers.

Table 118

Holidays[1] in Great Britain
1976

percentage

Destination[2]		Type of accommodation[3]	
One night or more spent in:			
Northumbria	2	Licensed hotel/motel	16
Yorkshire	7	Unlicensed hotel or	
East Midlands	4	guest house	11
East Anglia	10	Holiday camp	6
South East	13	Camping	7
Greater London	2	Caravan	20
Thames and Chilterns	2	Rented accommodation	11
South West	24	Paying guest	3
Heart of England	3	Home of friend or	
North West	7	relative	25
Cumbria	4	Other	5
Wales	15		
Scotland	11		

1. Holidays away from home of one night or more.
2. Figures add to more than 100% due to the inclusion of multi-destination trips.
3. Figures add to more than 100% because more than one type of accommodation was used on some holidays.

Table 119

**Economics of farming
United Kingdom**

Years June–May	£ million[1]	
	1970/71	1975/76
Output		
Farm crops[2]	444	1,211
Horticulture	277	551
Livestock and livestock products	1,639	3,512
Sundry outputs	12	34
Sundry receipts[3]	26	36
Production grants	116	113
Total receipts	2,514	5,456
Work in progress	+14	−50
Gross output	2,528	5,406
Input		
Feedingstuffs	637	1,242
Seeds	54	143
Livestock	76	123
Fertilizers and lime (before subsidy)	169	344
Machinery	181	383
Farm maintenance	100	178
Miscellaneous expenditure[4]	172	381
Total expenditure	1,389	2,794
Stock change	−3	+21
Gross input (total expenditure *less* change in stocks)	1,386	2,815
Gross product (gross output − gross input)	1,141	2,591
less Depreciation	195	523
Net product	946	2,068
less Labour, net rent and interest[5]	462	929
Farming net income (*less* stock appreciation)	484	1,139
Stock appreciation	+111	+537
Farming net income (including stock appreciation)	595	1,676

1. Valuation at current price.
2. Includes receipts from crops sold off farms, and subsequently bought back, cereal and potato seed, but excludes deficiency payments on retained cereals.
3. Deficiency payments on cereals retained, animal disease compensation, etc.
4. Electricity, veterinary expenses, pesticides, rates, etc.
5. Net rent = gross rent *less* landlord share of maintenance and depreciation. Interest on commercial debt for current farming purposes.

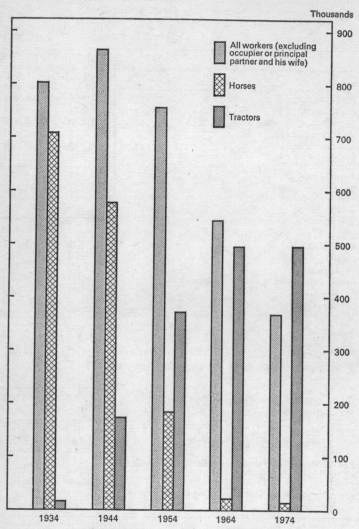

Thousands

All workers (excluding occupier or principal partner and his wife)

Horses

Tractors

Chart 23: Labour, horses and tractors employed in agriculture in Great Britain

Table 120

**Agricultural land
United Kingdom**

	At June		thousand hectares
	1966	1971[1]	1976[1]
Total agricultural area	19,588	19,115	18,987
Arable land	7,480	7,226	6,975
All grasses five years old and over[2]	4,937	4,926	5,081
Rough grazing (including common rough grazing)	7,170	6,678	6,513
Total woodland on agricultural holdings[3]	—	154	239
All other land on agricultural holdings[4]	—	131	180
Use of arable land	7,480	7,226	6,975
Wheat	906	1,097	1,231
Barley	2,481	2,288	2,182
Oats	367	363	235
Other cereals	33	63	37
Potatoes	271	256	222
Sugar beet	180	190	206
Fodder crops	313	276	285
Hops	8	7	6
Mustard	7	6	4
Fruit	96	80	68
Vegetables	147	183	206
Flowers and nursery stock	16	17	16
Other	7	12	59
Bare fallow	106	74	65
Lucerne	19	16	14
All grasses under five years old[5]	2,523	2,298	2,139

1. There was some change in June 1970 in the definition of agricultural holdings covered. This affects comparability with earlier years.
2. Before June 1975 collected as permanent grassland.
3. Before June 1974 collected as woodlands ancillary to farming.
4. Before June 1974 collected as other land used for agriculture.
5. Before June 1975 collected as temporary grassland.

Table 121
Crops harvested
United Kingdom

Years July–June

	Unit	1965/66	1970/71	1975/76
Wheat	Th. tonnes	4,171	4,236	4,489
yield per hectare	tonnes	4·07	4·20	4·34
Barley	Th. tonnes	8,192	7,529	8,511
yield per hectare	tonnes	3·75	3·36	3·63
Oats	Th. tonnes	1,233	1,217	795
yield per hectare	tonnes	3·02	3·25	3·42
Potatoes	Th. tonnes	7,577	7,482	4,551
yield per hectare	tonnes	25·3	27·6	22·3
Sugar beet	Th. tonnes	6,813	6,412	4,864
yield per hectare	tonnes	37·3	34·4	24·7
Turnips, swedes and fodder beet	Th. tonnes	6,612	5,651	6,035
yield per hectare	tonnes	49·4	56·3	56·5
Mangolds	Th. tonnes	1,536	580	411
yield per hectare	tonnes	64·3	59·7	59·6
Hay from all grasses under five years old[1]	Th. tonnes	4,721	4,286	3,757
yield per hectare	tonnes	4·39	4·33	4·27
Hay from all grasses five years old and over[2]	Th. tonnes	3,883	3,703	3,120
yield per hectare	tonnes	3·62	3·54	3·62

1. The 1965 and 1970 figures were collected as hay from temporary grassland but included hay from permanent grassland in Scotland; in 1975 the new definition shown above was adopted and figures include hay from all grasses five years old and over in Scotland.

2. The 1965 and 1970 figures were collected as hay from permanent grassland but excluded hay from permanent grassland in Scotland; in 1975 the new definition shown above was adopted and figures exclude hay from all grasses five years old and over in Scotland.

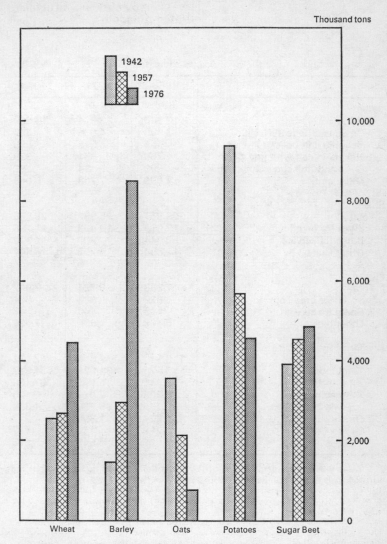

Thousand tons

1942
1957
1976

10,000

8,000

6,000

4,000

2,000

0

Wheat   Barley   Oats   Potatoes   Sugar Beet

**Chart 24: Crops harvested in
the United Kingdom**

Table 122

**Livestock on agricultural holdings
United Kingdom**

	At June		thousands
	1966	1971[1]	1976[1]
Cattle			
Total	12,206	12,804	14,069
Cows and heifers in milk	3,703	4,036	4,399
Cows in calf but not in milk	565	575	593
Heifers in calf with first calf	750	831	939
Bulls and bull calves for service	93	94	93
Other cattle	7,096	7,268	8,046
Sheep			
Total	29,957	25,981	28,265
Ewes for breeding	12,019	10,422	11,298
Rams for service	344	300	320
Other sheep	17,594	15,259	16,647
Pigs			
Total	7,333	8,724	7,947
Sows for breeding	822	984	884
Boars for service	43	46	43
Other pigs	6,468	7,695	7,020
Poultry			
Total	118,940	139,016	142,222
Total fowls	113,525	132,929	134,917
Laying flock	73,841	76,171	67,468
Breeding flock	6,908	7,029	6,125
Table birds	32,777	49,730	61,325
Ducks	1,227	1,395	1,272
Geese	219	143	127
Turkeys	3,968	4,548	5,905

1. There was some change in June 1970 in the definition of agricultural holdings covered. This affects comparability with 1966.

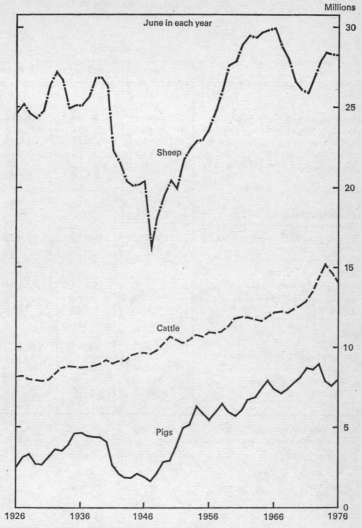

Millions

June in each year

Sheep

Cattle

Pigs

1926   1936   1946   1956   1966   1976

30

25

20

15

10

5

0

**Chart 25: Livestock in the
United Kingdom**

Table 123

Milk, eggs and wool: estimated production and utilization United Kingdom

June–May years

	Unit	1970/71	1975/76
Milk			
Average size of dairy herd	Thousands	3,284	3,237
Average gross yield per dairy cow	litres	3,851	4,301
Output for human consumption	Million litres	12,521	13,856
Consumed liquid[1]	Million litres	7,674	8,032
Manufactured into butter, cheese, etc.[2]	„ „	4,846	5,824
Fed to stock and waste[3]	„ „	257	183
Eggs (hen only)			
Average number of laying fowls	Thousands	66,601	58,306[5]
Average yield per layer	Eggs/bird	219·7	232·6[5]
Eggs gross production	Million dozen	1,219·2	1,130·1[5]
Utilization of output			
Output for human consumption	„ „	1,157·8	1,068·7[5]
Eggs used for hatching	„ „	49·3	50·2[5]
Waste	„ „	12·0	11·2[5]
Wool			
Sheep population at beginning of year	Thousands	26,080	28,270
Total wool production	million kgs	46·3	49·3
clip wool	(greasy)	32·1	35·1
skin wool[4]	„	14·2	14·3

1. Includes consumption in farm households.
2. Includes products manufactured on farms.
3. Dairy herd only.
4. Skin wool is the product of slaughtered sheep.
5. 366 days.

Table 124

Estimates of the proportion of UK food requirements derived from home agriculture and fisheries[1]

percentage

Years[2]	All food products		Indigenous food products only	
	Home output	Imports	Home output	Imports
1964/65	51·2	48·8	63·5	36·5
1965/66	50·2	49·8	62·9	37·1
1966/67	50·8	49·2	63·5	36·5
1967/68	51·6	48·4	64·6	35·4
1968/69	51·5	48·5	64·0	36·0
1969/70	52·4	47·6	64·7	35·3
1970/71	53·5	46·5	66·0	34·0
1971/72	53·9	46·1	67·0	33·0
1972/73	54·0	46·0	66·9	33·1
1973/74	56·0	44·0	69·8	30·2
1974/75	56·5	43·5	68·2	31·8
1975/76	52·2	47·8	63·8	36·2

1. At constant prices, 1970/71–1972/73 average.
2. Crop year June–May; imports July–June. For explanatory details see *Economic Trends*, November 1971.

Table 125

Index numbers of agricultural prices
United Kingdom
Average of 1968/69–1971/72 = 100[1]

	1971/72	1973/74	1975/76
Prices received by farmers (including subsidy, etc.)			
All products	107·2	157·1	230·7
Farm crops	103·5	169·7	311·4
Fatstock	110·4	161·3	223·0
Livestock products and poultry	107·0	149·7	200·5
Fruit and vegetables	104·1	147·1	217·9
Prices paid by farmers			
Feedingstuffs	106·1	196·2	221·8
Fertilizers	120·5	161·4	266·1
Lime	117·6	153·4	258·4
Fuel	109·1	142·8	228·7
Labour[2]	117·1	165·1	265·5

1. July–June years.
2. Great Britain only.

Table 126

**Fisheries
Great Britain**

Fishing fleet

number

	1966	1971	1976
Total vessels at 31 December	9,031	8,440	9,059
England and Wales	6,156	5,820	6,443
Scotland	2,875	2,620	2,616

Landing of fish of British taking

tonnes

	1966	1971	1976
Total landed weight (thousand tonnes)	943	964	917
Cod	325	305	211
Haddock	152	181	128
Herring	114	143	85
Plaice	40	44	32
Saithe (coalfish)	45	53	40
Shell fish	33	51	78
Other	234	187	343
Total value (£ thousand)	61,463	91,811	206,489
Cod	25,058	39,628	79,951
Haddock	10,830	17,288	34,858
Herring	2,851	4,849	10,846
Plaice	5,960	7,069	12,263
Saithe	1,576	2,957	6,970
Shell fish	3,482	6,985	21,539
Other	11,706	13,035	40,062

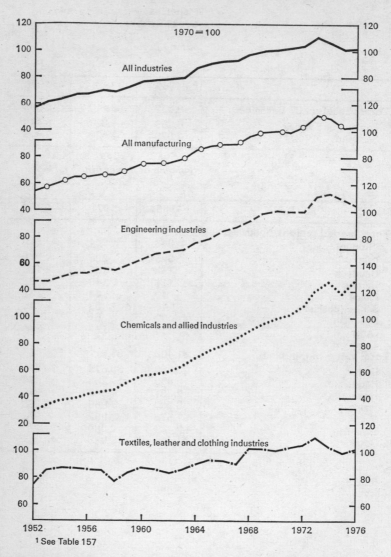

1970 = 100

All industries

All manufacturing

Engineering industries

Chemicals and allied industries

Textiles, leather and clothing industries

1952   1956   1960   1964   1968   1972   1976

[1] See Table 157

Chart 26: Index of industrial production United Kingdom[1]

Table 127

**Chemicals and allied trades:
production
United Kingdom**

	Unit	1966	1971	1976
Sulphuric acid	Thousand tonnes	3,168	3,459	3,271
Ethylene	" "	580	1,040	1,286
Propylene	" "	316	506	745
Benzene	" "	48	550	928
Ethyl alcohol	Million proof gallons	60	65	96[3]
Toilet preparations[1]	£ million	112	154	370
Paints and varnishes[1]	Million litres	372	463	585
Soap[2]	Thousand tonnes	344	260	..
Synthetic detergents[1]	" "	371	463	711
Synthetic resins: thermosetting	" "	316	370	442
thermoplastic	" "	685	1,061	2,068
Plastic materials: thermosetting	" "	94	101	264
thermoplastic	" "	226	321	368
Synthetic rubber	" "	194	286	320
Synthetic dyestuffs	Million kgs	..	..	53
Fertilizers:				
Phosphatic (P_2O_5 content)	Thousand tonnes	427	539	393
Nitrogenous (N content)	" "	665	748	821
Potassic (K_2O content) (home deliveries)	" "	418	493	414
Compounds (total weight)	" "	2,754	3,005	2,855

1. Net sales by firms employing 25 or more persons.
2. Deliveries by firms employing 25 or more persons.
3. Provisional.

Table 128

Iron and steel
United Kingdom

	1966	1971	1976[1]
Iron			
Number of blast furnaces in existence at end of period	82	61	52
Iron ore production (thousand tonnes)	13,877	10,228	4,585
Pig iron production (thousand tonnes)	15,962	15,416	13,833
Steel			
Number of steel furnaces in existence at end of period	724	610	534
Total supply of steel (thousand tonnes ingot equivalent)	26,570	27,620	25,974
Home sources:			
Total	25,380	24,940	20,545
Crude steel production	24,700	24,170	22,274[2]
Re-usable material[3]	250	180	88
Deliveries to (−) or from (+) stocks[4]	+430	+590	−1,815
Imported	1,190	2,680	5,429
Distribution of supply (thousand tonnes ingot equivalent)			
Exports	4,530	6,380	4,805
Supply for home use	22,040	21,240	21,169
Net deliveries − actual tonnage (thousand tonnes)[5]			
Exports	3,337	4,516	3,234
For home use	15,921	16,111	16,130

Figures of imports and exports are based on statistics as shown in *Overseas Trade Statistics of the United Kingdom*.

1. Provisional.
2. On 1 January 1976, the UK definition of crude steel was revised to agree with the Community definition. Continuously cast steel, which was previously recorded in liquid form, is now recorded at the first stage of solidification. The difference is comparatively minor and reduces the figure by about 0·5 per cent.
3. Second-hand tubes, and other finished steel and old rails for re-rolling.
4. Stocks at producers' works of ingots and semi-finished steel, but excluding stocks held by consumers and stock holding merchants.
5. Finished steel, excluding deliveries of all material for intra-industry conversion.

Table 129

**Non-ferrous metals
United Kingdom**

thousand tonnes

	1966	1971	1976
Copper			
Production of refined copper	180	178	137
Home consumption (refined and scrap)	743	645	605
Zinc			
Production of slab zinc	101	117	42
Home consumption (slab and scrap)	355	358	308
Lead			
Production of refined lead	113	143	119
Home consumption (refined and scrap)	414	346	301
Tin			
Production of tin metal	19	25	13
Home consumption (excluding scrap)	20	18	15
Aluminium			
Production	235	308	540
Home consumption	565	539	780

Table 130

**Deliveries of radios, electronic
apparatus, domestic electrical
appliances and selected
engineering products
United Kingdom**

	1966	1971	1976[1]
Radios and electronic apparatus (thousands)			
Radio sets	1,061	830	728
Car radios	335	551	319
Radiograms	182	206	31
Record players	403	523	218
Television sets:			
Monochrome	} 1,365 {	1,583	1,544
Colour		834	860
Gramophone records	84,871	120,524	176,769
Domestic electrical appliances (thousands)			
Blankets and pads	1,507	1,359	1,394
Cookers	546	823	716
Floor polishers	73	76	73
Irons	2,407	2,217	2,772
Refrigerators, refrigerator/freezers	984	1,013	1,371
Deep-freeze units	..	..	261
Vacuum cleaners	1,540	2,162	2,839
Washing machines, domestic	702	1,049	1,244
Electrical machinery (£ million)			
Transformers for lighting, heating and power	69·1	54·7	101·5
Switchgear and control gear	197·9	191·3	310·5
Insulated wires and cables	253·6	338·1	581·7
Telegraph and telephone apparatus	146·9	288·5	538·9
Radio, radar and electronic capital equipment (£ million)			
Electronic control equipment	49·4	87·4	..[2]
Electronic computers	74·8	193·4	629·4
Electronic measuring and testing equipment	31·3	49·1	80·4
Radar and navigational aids	79·6	110·6	244·7
Radio communications equipment	42·2	70·7	191·1

1. Provisional.
2. Series ceased 1972.

Table 131

**Merchant shipbuilding
United Kingdom**

Vessels of 100 gross tons and over

		1966	1971	1976
Completions				
Value (£ million):	Total	140	180	375
	For export	34	51	144
Number of vessels:	Total	211	134	140
	For export	38	38	43
Net new orders				
Value (£ million):	Total	69	122	104
	For export	33	104	145
Number of vessels:	Total	145	54	87
	For export	34	17	38
Orders on hand[1]				
Value (£ million):	Total	267	678	1,057
	For export	106	219	364
Number of vessels				
under construction:	Total	164	141	119
	For export	47	24	33
not yet laid down:	Total	90	115	85
	For export	35	35	35

1. At end of year.

Table 132

**New aircraft, motor vehicles
and cycles: production
United Kingdom**

thousands

	1966	1971	1976
New aircraft (deliveries number)	431	380	341
Motor vehicles[1]			
Passenger cars			
Total	1,603·7	1,741·9	1,333·5
1,000 cc and under	301·4	272·1	134·7
Over 1,000 cc to 1,600 cc	813·8	972·8	736·0
Over 1,600 cc to 2,800 cc	412·5	425·0	404·7
Over 2,800 cc	75·9	72·0	58·0
Commercial vehicles			
Total	438·7	380·7	372·1
Buses and coaches	24·2	35·6	33·2
Goods vehicles	414·4	345·1	338·9
Motor cycles, mopeds and motor scooters (deliveries)	94·8	44·1[2]	12·6[3]
Pedal cycles (deliveries)	1,423	1,769	1,833[3]

1. Figures for cars include taxis; chassis delivered as such by the manufacturers
are included with both cars and commercial vehicles.
2. 1972 figure.
3. Provisional.

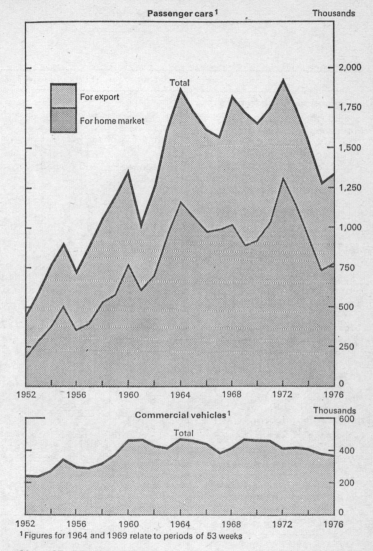

Passenger cars[1]

Thousands

For export

For home market

Total

Commercial vehicles[1]

Thousands

Total

[1] Figures for 1964 and 1969 relate to periods of 53 weeks

**Chart 27: Motor vehicle
production
United Kingdom**

Table 133

Textiles
United Kingdom

	Unit	1966	1971	1976
Cotton and man-made fibres				
Imports of raw cotton	Th. tonnes	291	205	177
Production of cotton yarn (including waste yarn)	Million kgs	207	133	107
Production of cotton cloth	Mn lin. metres	837	559	375
Production of man-made fibres	Th. tonnes	400	613	618
Production of spun man-made fibre and mixture yarn (including waste yarn)	Million kgs	62	83	76
Production of man-made fibre and mixture cloth	Mn lin. metres	564	480	493
Wool				
Virgin wool (clean weight):				
Imports	Million kgs	161	114	114
Home production	„	39	31	32
Production of tops:				
Wool and hair	„	104	66	56
Man-made fibre	„	28	37	47
Deliveries of worsted yarn[1]	„	100	84	72
Production of woollen yarn[1]	„	143	131	108
Deliveries of woven fabrics (woollen and worsted excluding blankets)[1]	Mn sq. metres	253	186	143
Deliveries of blankets	„	26	28	23
Other textile industries				
Manufacturers' sales				
Weft knitted fabrics	Mn sq. metres	147	285	315
Warp knitted fabrics	£ million	32	67	86
Knitted garments	„	125	219	412
Socks and stockings including tights and pantihose	„	74	96	136
Woven wool carpets	Mn sq. yds	39	38	29
Tufted carpets	„	43	85	150
Other carpets and rugs	„	21	36	30

1. Includes man-made fibres and mixtures.

Table 134

**Woodpulp, paper and
paper-making materials
United Kingdom**

thousand tonnes

	1966	1971	1976
Woodpulp Consumption for papermaking	2,541	2,144	1,720
Other paper-making materials[1] Consumption (paper equivalent)	1,726	2,044	2,149
Newsprint Production	749	575	326
Home consumption	1,423	1,369	1,280
Other paper and board[2] Production	3,851	3,792	3,856

1. Includes pulpwood, rags, waste rope, etc.
2. For example food wrappings, household toilet papers and tissues, packaging board.

Table 135

**Alcoholic drink
United Kingdom**

	1966	1971	1976
Spirits (million proof gallons) Produced	145·1	161·7	153·9[2]
Consumed	17·8	20·8	35·6
Beer (million bulk barrels)[1] Produced	30·2	34·7	40·1
Consumed	30·8	35·8	40·7
Wine (million gallons) Consumed	37·7	53·9	80·7

1. A bulk barrel is 36 gallons.
2. Provisional.

Table 136
Construction industries
Great Britain

Value of output

£ million

	1966	1971	1976
All work: Total[1]	4,335·6	6,116·3	12,526·7
New work: Total[1]	3,098·1	4,421·9	8,765·5
New housing: Total	1,246·1	1,628·4	3,588·2
For public sector	594·2	687·6	1,797·9
For private sector	651·9	940·8	1,790·4
Other new work: Total[2]	1,852·0	2,793·5	5,177·2
For public sector	881·8	1,452·4	2,741·6
For private sector	970·2	1,341·1	2,435·6
of which: Industrial	505·6	658·4	1,210·8
Commercial	464·6	682·7	1,224·8
Repair and maintenance	1,237·5	1,694·4	3,761·2

1. Output by contractors, including unrecorded estimates by small firms and self-employed workers, and by the public sectors' direct labour departments classified to construction in the 1968 Standard Industrial Classification.
2. Series revised by removing output of some firms, e.g. those producing steel oil-drilling platforms, now classified under 'Structural steel fabrication', not 'Construction'.

Production of building materials

	Unit	1966	1971	1976[1]
Building bricks (GB)	Millions	7,072	6,541	5,406
Cement (UK)	Mn tonnes	16·8	17·7	15·8
Plasterboard (GB)	Mn sq. m	64·7	95·4	117·0
Sand and gravel (GB)	Mn tonnes	105·2	111·8	110·4[2]
Ready mixed concrete (UK)	Mn cu. m	16·6	25·2	24·8

1. Figures of output include additional sites, the effect of which has been to increase production by an average of:
   1% for building bricks,
   11% for sand and gravel,
   3% for ready mixed concrete.
2. Provisional.

Table 137

**Index numbers of wholesale prices
United Kingdom**

1970 = 100

Input prices

Annual averages

	1971	1975	1976
Materials and fuel purchased by manufacturing industry	104·6	235·5	299·0
Materials and fuel purchased by selected broad sectors of industry			
Food manufacturing industries	107·1	201·6	257·6
Chemicals and allied industries	108·8	239·1	283·8
Steel industries	110·3	226·1	279·8
Mechanical engineering industries	107·9	208·1	251·8
Electrical engineering industries	100·5	179·3	221·1
Textile industries	104·8	201·7	265·5
Clothing and footwear industries	105·7	182·4	214·1
Construction materials	109·1	205·7	249·8
House building materials	110·1	207·5	252·9

Output prices

Annual averages

	1971	1975	1976
Output of manufactured products	109·0	188·7	219·6
Output of selected broad sectors of industry			
Products of the food manufacturing industries	109·1	200·1	228·4
Chemicals and allied industries	108·2	188·7	217·5
Steel industries	109·1	226·7	269·9
Mechanical engineering industries	110·6	196·6	231·2
Electrical engineering industries	108·1	173·2	202·6
Textile industries	104·9	178·6	205·9
Clothing and footwear industries	106·5	163·6	184·2
New construction[1]	106·9	223·4	257·6[2]

1. Index of building costs.
2. Provisional.

Table 138

**Inland energy consumption
United Kingdom**

Heat supplied basis

million therms[1]

	1966	1971	1976
Gross consumption of primary fuels: *of which*	76,803	82,741	81,709
Coal	45,565	34,828	29,780
Petroleum	28,597	37,994	33,758
Nuclear and hydro-electricity	2,323	2,686	3,408
Natural gas	318	7,233	14,763
Less energy used by fuel industries and losses in distribution	23,238	25,739	24,380
Total consumption by final users	53,565	57,002	57,329
Type of fuel consumed:			
Coal (direct use)	16,122	9,867	6,022
Coke and breeze	6,032	4,023	3,182
Other solid fuel	623	926	703
Coke oven gas	483	444	433
Town gas	3,685	3,526	212
Natural gas (direct use)	—	3,744	13,182
Electricity	5,222	6,757	7,358
Petroleum (direct use)	21,034	27,617	26,193
Other fuels (direct use)	364	98	44
Class of consumer:			
Domestic	14,407	14,141	14,546
Transport	9,604	11,634	12,716
Iron and steel industry	6,849	6,561	5,302
Other industries	16,230	17,506	17,525
Other final consumers	6,475	7,160	7,240

1. For conversion factors see *Digest of United Kingdom Energy Statistics, 1977.*

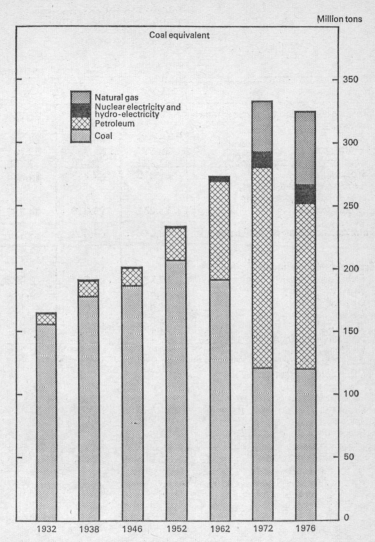

Million tons

Coal equivalent

Natural gas
Nuclear electricity and
hydro-electricity
Petroleum
Coal

1932   1938   1946   1952   1962   1972   1976

*Chart 28: Total inland energy
consumption
United Kingdom*

Table 139

**Coal production at
National Coal Board mines
Great Britain**

Years ended March

	1971/72		1976/77	
	Output[1]	Output per man-shift	Output[1]	Output per man-shift
	Million tons	cwt	Million tons	cwt
All NCB mines	109·2	41·9	106·7	43·6
Scottish	10·4	38·1	9·0	38·6
North East	15·5	34·9	12·9	36·4
North Yorkshire	8·4	54·9	8·1	50·6
Doncaster	6·8	45·4	7·7	48·2
Barnsley	6·7	43·6	7·2	44·4
South Yorkshire	7·6	42·7	7·6	43·1
North Derbyshire	7·6	57·3	7·2	55·6
North Nottingham	9·6	54·2	10·5	56·9
South Nottingham	8·4	54·3	8·9	54·1
South Midlands[2]	7·8	48·3	8·7	51·1
Western	10·7	37·6	11·2	43·0
South Wales	9·7	28·1	7·7	25·9

1. Excludes coal extracted in work on capital account (0·1 million tons in 1976/77).
2. Includes Kent coalfield.

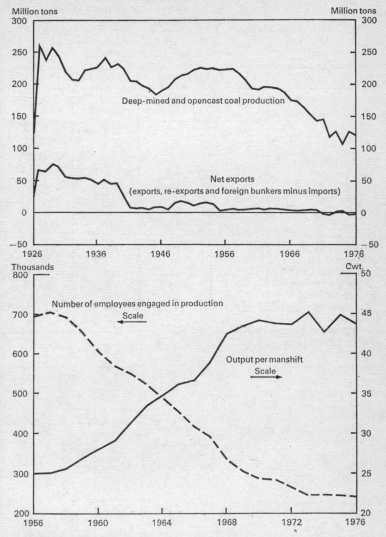

Million tons

Deep-mined and opencast coal production

Net exports
(exports, re-exports and foreign bunkers minus imports)

Number of employees engaged in production
Scale

Output per manshift
Scale

Thousands

Cwt.

**Chart 29: Coal production
and exports
Great Britain**

Table 140

Electricity: production, sales and manpower employed United Kingdom

	Unit	1966	1971	1976
Electricity generated	TWh[1]	184·8	236·4	255·6
Method of generation				
Steam plant (nuclear)	"	17·8	23·2	32·4
Steam plant (other)	"	162·3	208·5	218·2
Oil engines	"	0·8	1·0	0·5
Water power	"	3·9	3·7	4·5
Fuel used				
Coal	Million tons	68·4	71·6	76·4
Coke and coke breeze	"	0·6	0·1	0·1
Oil	"	7·3	14·5	10·0
Natural gas	Mn therms	—	263	662
Sales	TWh[1]			
Premises:				
Domestic and farm	"	63·0	84·4	88·7
Combined domestic and commercial	"	2·3	2·8	2·5
Shops, offices and other commercial	"	23·1	31·9	37·4
Factories and other industrial	"	67·8	80·3	87·7
Public lighting	"	1·3	1·8	2·2
Traction	"	2·5	2·8	2·9
		160·0	204·0	221·4
		1966/67[2]	1971/72[2]	1975/76[2]
Manpower				
Average number of persons employed	Thousands	255	206	195
Operatives	"	169	120	108
Administrative, technical and clerical	"	86	86	87
Wages and salaries				
Total	£ million	270	351	661
Operatives	"	162	194	334
Administrative, technical and clerical	"	108	157	327

1. 1 terawatt hour (TWh) = 1,000,000,000 kilowatt hours (KWh).
2. Year ended March.

Table 141

Gas: production, sales and manpower employed
United Kingdom

	Unit	1966	1971	1976
Production				
Gas available at gas works	Mn therms	4,054	8,082	14,499
Gas made at gas works	„ „	2,573	849	67
Gas bought:				
from coke ovens	„ „	418	222	9
from oil refineries	„ „	799	326	30
natural gas	„ „	264	6,685	14,393
Fuel used at gas works				
Coal	Th. tons	16,818	1,770	8
Oil	„ „	5,329	1,881	181
Sales				
Total	Mn therms	3,685	7,520	13,997
Domestic	„ „	2,177	3,930	6,194
Industrial	„ „	932	2,724	6,282
Commercial, public administration and lighting	„ „	576	866	1,521
		1966/ 67[1]	1971/ 72[1]	1975/ 76[1]
Manpower				
Average number of persons employed	Thousands	125	116	104
Operatives	„	74	53	42
Administrative, technical and clerical	„	51	63	62
Wages and salaries				
Total	£ million	124	185	329
Operatives	„	70	81	134
Administrative, technical and clerical	„	54	104	195

1. Year ended March.

Table 142

Licences issued for natural gas and oil and results obtained
United Kingdom

		1971		1976	
	Unit	Land	Off-shore	Land	Off-shore
Number of exclusive licences[1]	Number	181	110	136	181
Total area licensed[1]	Th. sq. kms	69·0	56·4	45·1	88·4
Wells drilled[2]					
Production	Number	—	37	—	59
Exploration/appraisal	„	12	29	6	104
Total depth drilled	Th. kms	15·5	170·7	7·8	449·6
Production					
Gas	Mn cu. m	177	18,285	4	38,499
Natural gas liquids	Th. tonnes	2	127	—	376
Oil	„ „	83	—	99	11,531

1. At end of year.
2. Includes those being drilled at end of year.

Table 143

**Petroleum: UK imports
of crude and process oils**

By countries of origin

	Quantity: million tons			Value: £ million c.i.f.[1]		
	1966	1971	1976	1966	1971	1976
Total imports	70·2	107·6	87·3	426	956	4,586
Middle East						
Kuwait	15·6	21·4	11·3	87	184	578
Iran	4·3	10·6	19·6	26	94	1,020
Iraq	10·3	3·9	5·2	63	34	276
Saudi Arabia	6·5	21·0	18·3	39	172	950
Other Middle East	4·5	9·7	10·1	28	86	525
Western Hemisphere						
Venezuela	6·3	6·5	1·5	38	56	63
Other Western Hemisphere	2·2	0·4	0·4	15	6	24
Other countries						
Libya	10·0	20·2	2·2	60	191	123
Nigeria	7·0	8·9	3·8	43	83	204
All other countries	3·5	5·0	14·9	27	50	323

1. Cost, insurance and freight.

Table 144

**Refinery throughput of crude
and process oils, and output
of refined products
United Kingdom**

million tonnes

	1966	1971	1974	1975	1976
Throughput of crude and process oils	71·7	105·3	111·2	93·5	97·8
Refinery fuel and losses	5·4	7·1	8·1	6·9	7·5
Total output of refined products	**66·3**	**98·2**	**103·1**	**86·6**	**90·3**
Gases	1·6	1·5	1·9	1·6	1·7
Naphtha	4·0	5·7	6·4	4·0	4·6
Motor spirit	8·8	12·5	14·5	13·9	15·2
Gas/Diesel oil	14·9	24·5	27·6	23·3	24·2
Fuel oil	29·1	43·2	40·0	32·7	32·7
Lubricating oil	1·1	1·4	1·5	1·1	1·3
Bitumen	1·6	2·1	2·1	2·1	1·9
Other products	5·2	7·3	9·1	7·9	8·7

Table 145

Fuel prices and selling values

All classes of consumer
Great Britain

	1965/66	1970/71	1975/76
Proceeds per ton of saleable mined coal (pence)	458	584	1,609
	1966	1971	1976
Average net selling value of electricity per kWh sold (pence)	0·734	0·849	1·899
	1965/66	1970/71	1975/76
Average net selling value of gas per therm (pence)	9·32	8·70	9·87

Index of retail prices
United Kingdom
15 January 1974 = 100

	1971	1972	1973	1974	1975	1976
Coal and coke	83	92	95	106	141	175
Gas	93	98	99	104	120	147
Electricity	87	92	94	115	166	207
Fuel and light total (including oil)	85·3	91·9	94·5	110·7	147·4	182·4

Index numbers of wholesale prices
1970 = 100

	1971	1972	1973	1974	1975	1976
Motor spirit produced in the United Kingdom – two star (including duty)	105·0	106·6	111·5	146·5	173·2	203·9

Table 146

**Retail distribution and service
trades: shops
Great Britain**

thousands

	1961	1966	1971
Retail trade			
Total retail shops	542·3	504·4	473·0
Co-operative societies	29·4	26·7	15·4
Multiples (other retail organizations with 10 or more establishments)	66·7	73·9	66·8
Independents (retail organizations with fewer than 10 establishments)	446·2	403·9	390·8
Grocers and provision dealers	146·8	123·4	105·3
Other food retailers	114·7	104·4	92·5
Confectioners, tobacconists, newsagents	70·1	63·3	52·1
Clothing and footwear shops	86·6	83·1	81·3
Household goods shops	60·3	65·9	70·3
Other non-food retailers	60·1	61·4	66·7
General stores	3·8	3·0	4·8
Not included above:			
Market stalls and mobile shops	35·0	..	31·8
Electricity and Gas Board showrooms	2·8	3·0	2·4
Mail order businesses (organizations)	0·56	0·50	0·77
Automatic vending machine operators (organizations)	0·03	0·06	0·07
Service trades			
Footwear repairing establishments	11·2	8·8	5·5
Hairdressing establishments	40·2	47·6	47·2
Laundries, launderette operators and dry cleaners (organizations)	4·6	5·6	8·4

The 1961 and 1966 figures have been adjusted to correspond as far as possible
with the 1971 figures and they thus differ slightly from those published in the
report on the 1966 Census of Distribution. These differences arise from changes in
scope, presentation and classification. Figures for all 3 years exclude market traders
and mobile shops other than those traders operating from fixed lockable premises
in permanent markets and the market stalls and mobile shops operated by
co-operative societies and multiple shop retailers.

Table 147

Retail distribution and service trades: turnover
Great Britain

£ million

	1961	1966	1971
Retail trade			
Total retail shops	8,828	11,132	15,611
Co-operative societies	959	1,016	1,108
Multiples (other retail organizations with 10 or more establishments)	2,579	3,837	6,084
Independents (retail organizations with fewer than 10 establishments)	5,290	6,279	8,419
Grocers and provision dealers	2,351	2,908	4,156
Other food retailers	1,728	2,081	2,615
Confectioners, tobacconists, newsagents	798	1,046	1,306
Clothing and footwear shops	1,367	1,719	2,372
Household goods shops	948	1,292	2,007
Other non-food retailers	707	1,019	1,569
General stores	930	1,067	1,587
Not included above:			
Market stalls and mobile shops	91	..	147
Electricity and Gas Board showrooms[1]	104	186	283
Mail order businesses (organizations)	227	429	633
Automatic vending machine operators (organizations)	4	11	12
Service trades			
Footwear repairing establishments	25	26	22
Hairdressing establishments	91	136	166
Laundries, launderette operators and dry cleaners (organizations)	112	172	212

The 1961 and 1966 figures have been adjusted to correspond as far as possible with the 1971 figures and they thus differ slightly from those published in the report on the 1966 Census of Distribution. These differences arise from changes in scope, presentation and classification. Figures for all 3 years exclude market traders and mobile shops other than those traders operating from fixed lockable premises in permanent markets and the market stalls and mobile shops operated by co-operative societies and multiple shop retailers.

1. 1961 figures exclude, and 1966 and 1971 figures include, charges for the installation, maintenance and repair of appliances.

Table 148

Retail distribution and service trades: persons engaged Great Britain

thousands

	1961	1966	1971
Retail trade			
Total retail shops	2,485	2,556	2,541
Co-operative societies	195	173	132
Multiples (other retail organizations with 10 or more establishments)	633	742	815
Independents (retail organizations with fewer than 10 establishments)	1,657	1,640	1,595
Grocers and provision dealers	552	522	543
Other food retailers	472	459	418
Confectioners, tobacconists, newsagents	250	298	275
Clothing and footwear shops	397	411	404
Household goods shops	265	290	290
Other non-food retailers	237	270	298
General stores	313	306	313
Not included above:			
Market stalls and mobile shops	39	..	38
Electricity and Gas Board showrooms	..	..	11
Mail-order businesses (organizations)	41	55	60
Automatic vending machine operators (organizations)	1	2	2
Service trades			
Footwear repairing establishments	24	19	11
Hairdressing establishments	139	163	155
Laundries, launderette operators and dry cleaners	137	141	115

The 1961 and 1966 figures have been adjusted to correspond as far as possible with the 1971 figures and they thus differ slightly from those published in the report on the 1966 Census of Distribution. These differences arise from changes in scope, presentation and classsification. Figures for all 3 years exclude market traders and mobile shops other than those traders operating from fixed lockable premises in permanent markets and the market stalls and mobile shops operated by co-operative societies and multiple shop retailers.

Table 149
Wholesale trades
Great Britain

1965

	Business units	Turnover	Persons engaged (full- and part-time)
	Number	£ million	Thousands
Total	41,049	14,771	779
Wholesale distribution : total	23,643	8,771	463
Food and drink	2,007	1,999	67
Clothing and textiles	2,630	468	38
Hardware and electrical goods	3,195	467	41
Other	2,400	385	40
	13,411	5,452	277
Dealing in coal, oil, builders' materials, grain and agricultural supplies : total	8,282	2,308	148
Coal and oil merchants	4,291	814	45
Builders' merchants	2,308	649	68
Agriculture and livestock	1,683	845	35
Dealing in other industrial materials and machinery	9,117	3,235	164
Marketing Boards	7	457	4

Table 150
Catering trades
Great Britain

	Establishments		Organizations[1]			
	1969	1969	1969	1969	1971	1976
	Thou-sands	Turn-over £ million	Thou-sands	Turnover £ million		
Total (excluding clubs)	131·7	2,517	111·6	2,533	3,000	5,818
Licensed hotels, motels, licensed guest houses and holiday camps	8·0	445	6·8	408	503	1,047
Restaurants, cafes, snack bars and fish and chip shops	44·0	624	42·2	623	701	1,240
Public houses	61·3	1,308	48·1	1,349	1,636	3,239
Canteens	18·3	140	14·5	153	160	292
Clubs						
Licensed	2·5	64	2·5	64	..	..
Registered	23·4	372	23·4	372	..	..

1. Turnover of organizations excludes transactions between establishments within the same organization.

Table 151

Motor trades
Great Britain

	Establishments		Organizations[1]	
	1972		1972	
	Thou-sands	Turnover £ million	Thou-sands	Turnover £ million
Total	55·1	8,102	46·1	8,109
New vehicle dealers	9·9	5,055	8·3	5,231
Concessionaires of foreign manufacture of vehicles or motor cycles	0·3	479	0·3	487
Vehicle distributors/main dealers	4·7	3,283	3·5	3,462
Other new vehicle dealers	4·9	1,293	4·5	1,282
Motor cycle dealers (new and/or used)	1·6	92	1·5	89
Used vehicle dealers	5·3	519	5·0	490
General repairers (including servicing)	13·3	514	12·9	482
Specialist repairers (e.g. bodywork, electrical)	4·1	117	3·9	106
Retail dealers in motor parts and/or accessories	4·0	161	2·7	156
Wholesale dealers in motor parts and/or accessories	1·9	280	1·0	264
Tyre and/or battery dealers	3·1	304	1·4	286
Petrol stations	11·2	981	9·1	926
Caravan dealers	0·6	79	0·5	80

1. Turnover of organizations excludes transactions between establishments within the same organization.

XV National income and expenditure

Table 152
Gross domestic and national product
United Kingdom

£ million

	1966	1971	1976
Expenditure			
Consumers' expenditure	24,260	35,399	73,656
General government final consumption	6,502	10,212	26,562
Gross domestic fixed capital formation	6,922	10,515	23,427
Value of physical increase in stocks and work in progress	342	110	359
Total domestic expenditure at market prices	38,026	56,236	124,004
Exports of goods and services	7,137	12,881	34,837
less Imports of goods and services	−7,218	−12,110	−36,564
less Taxes on expenditure	−5,421	−8,787	−16,660
Subsidies	559	931	3,463
Gross domestic product at factor cost	33,083	49,151	109,080
Factor incomes			
Income from employment	22,814	33,659	78,639
Income from self-employment[1]	2,671	4,383	10,208
Gross trading profits of companies[1,3]	4,592	6,695	12,445
Gross trading surplus of public corporations[1]	1,042	1,520	4,460
Gross trading surplus of other public enterprises[1]	106	177	120
Rent[2]	1,822	3,162	7,771
Imputed charge for consumption of non-trading capital	233	377	1,012
Total domestic income	33,280	49,973	114,655
less Stock appreciation	−360	−1,090	−6,557
Residual error	163	268	982
Gross domestic product at factor cost	33,083	4,915	109,080
Net property income from abroad	387	505	1,179
Gross national product	33,470	49,656	110,259
less Capital consumption	−3,090	−5,082	−13,583
National income	30,380	44,574	96,676

1. Before providing for depreciation and stock appreciation.
2. Before providing for depreciation.
3. Including financial institutions.

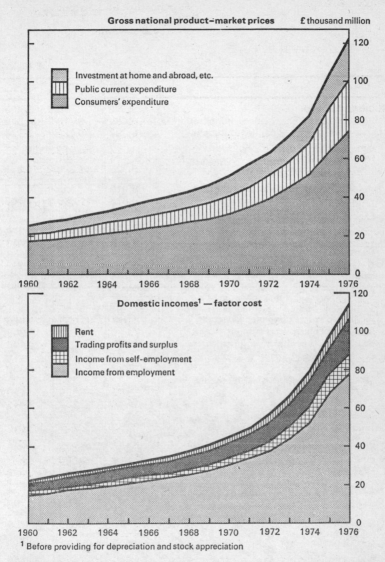

Gross national product—market prices £ thousand million

Investment at home and abroad, etc.
Public current expenditure
Consumers' expenditure

Domestic incomes[1] — factor cost

Rent
Trading profits and surplus
Income from self-employment
Income from employment

[1] Before providing for depreciation and stock appreciation

***Chart 30: Gross national product
United Kingdom***

Table 153

**Expenditure and output at
1970 prices
United Kingdom**

£ million

	1966	1971	1976
Consumers' expenditure	29,280	32,675	35,405
General government final consumption	8,489	9,228	11,049
Gross domestic fixed capital formation	8,097	9,682	9,724
Value of physical increase in stocks and work in progress	424	92	66
Exports of goods and services	8,725	12,308	15,369
Total final expenditure at market prices	55,015	63,985	71,613
less Imports of goods and services[1]	−8,873	−11,659	−14,207
Gross domestic product at market prices[2]	46,142	52,326	57,406
less Adjustment to factor cost	−6,918	−7,817	−9,012
Gross domestic product at factor cost[3]	39,224	44,509	48,394

1. Excluding taxes on expenditure levied on imports.
2. Including taxes on expenditure levied on imports.
3. This represents taxes on expenditure *less* subsidies valued at constant rates.

Table 154

**Growth of gross domestic
product at factor cost
United Kingdom**
1970 = 100

	1966	1971	1976
At current prices			
Based on expenditure data	76·3	113·3	251·5
Based on income data	75·3	111·8	247·2
At 1970 prices			
Based on expenditure data	90·4	102·6	111·6
Based on income data	89·3	101·2	109·7
Based on output data	90·9	101·5	108·9
Average estimate	90·2	101·8	110·1

Table 155

Gross domestic product per head, by region

Factor cost, current prices

£

	1966	1971	1975
United Kingdom	605	877	1,647
England — North	516	766	1,571
Yorkshire and Humberside	592	819	1,597
East Midlands	590	847	1,612
East Anglia	584	822	1,510
South East	683	999	1,858
South West	558	815	1,504
West Midlands	662	903	1,614
North West	584	846	1,590
All English regions	624	898	1,681
Wales	516	775	1,446
Scotland	543	806	1,584
Northern Ireland	412	653	1,207

Table 156

**Gross domestic product
by industry[1]
United Kingdom**

	1966	1971	1976
£ million			
Agriculture, forestry and fishing	1,061	1,359	3,116
Mining and quarrying	689	683	2,458
Manufacturing	11,003	15,562	30,464
Construction	2,261	3,192	7,793
Gas, electricity and water	1,069	1,574	3,905
Transport	2,079	3,018	6,624
Communication	703	1,190	3,691
Distributive trades	3,756	5,246	10,379
Insurance, banking and finance	1,929	3,582	7,717
Ownership of dwellings	1,535	2,636	6,723
Public administration and defence	2,095	3,463	8,458
Public health and educational services	1,646	2,757	8,055
Other services	4,037	6,139	13,417
Total	33,863	50,401	112,750
Adjustment for financial services	−943	−1,518	−4,702
Residual error	163	268	982
Gross domestic product at factor cost	33,083	49,151	109,080
As a percentage			
Agriculture, forestry and fishing	3·1	2·7	2·8
Mining and quarrying	2·0	1·4	2·2
Manufacturing	32·5	30·9	27·0
Construction	6·7	6·3	6·9
Gas, electricity and water	3·2	3·1	3·5
Transport	6·1	6·0	5·9
Communication	2·1	2·4	3·3
Distributive trades	11·1	10·4	9·2
Insurance, banking and finance	5·7	7·1	6·8
Ownership of dwellings	4·5	5·2	6·0
Public administration and defence	6·2	6·9	7·5
Public health and educational services	4·9	5·5	7·1
Other services	11·9	12·1	11·1
Total	100·0	100·0	100·0

1. After deducting stock appreciation.

Table 157

**Index numbers of output at
constant factor cost
United Kingdom**
1970 = 100

	1966	1971	1976
Agriculture, forestry and fishing	91	106	101
Industrial production:			
Mining and quarrying	115·3	100·0	89·2
Manufacturing			
Food, drink and tobacco	91·3	100·6	110·6
Coal and petroleum products	79·7	103·3	96·3
Chemicals and allied industries	78·8	102·1	128·4
Metal manufacture	97·7	91·3	85·2
Mechanical engineering	87·8	98	97·3
Instrument engineering	75·0	103·3	114·3
Electrical engineering	82·4	101·7	110·6
Shipbuilding and marine engineering	92·1	98·7	88·9
Vehicles	96·3	100·2	96·8
Metal goods not elsewhere specified	94·1	93·3	93·6
Textiles	85·9	100·6	97·3
Leather, leather goods and fur	107·7	103·0	95·3
Clothing and footwear	100·9	105·4	111·1
Bricks, pottery, glass, cement, etc.	94·1	108·1	110·4
Timber, furniture, etc.	95·9	103	111·1
Paper, printing and publishing	92·8	97·3	97·6
Other manufacturing industries	81·9	99·8	114·5
Total manufacturing	89·2	99·5	103·4
Construction	96·7	103·1	88·9
Gas, electricity and water	83·0	103·9	123·9
Total industrial production	90·6	100·3	102·2
Transport and communication	88	101	116
Distributive trades	92	101	111
Insurance, banking, finance and business services	82	107	131
Ownership of dwellings	90	102	113
Professional and scientific services	89	103	124
Miscellaneous services	98	103	108
Public administration and defence	99	101	108
Adjustment for financial services	84	108	136
Gross domestic product[1]	90·9	101·5	108·9

1. For 1971 and 1976 the gross domestic product is shown adjusted to allow
for the use of delivery rather than production indicators to represent output in
certain industries within manufacturing. The industrial production index and the
index for manufacturing are not adjusted for this effect.

Table 158
**Central government current
account: revenue
United Kingdom**

£ million

	1966	1971	1976
Taxes on income			
Income tax	4,236	6,090	16,582
Surtax	210	86	87
Profits tax	135	1	—
Corporation tax	23	1,535	2,081
less Overspill relief	−38	−28	−26
Total taxes on income	4,566	7,884	18,724
Taxes on expenditure			
Customs and Excise duties:			
Beer	361	479	773
Wines and spirits	314	499	1,116
Tobacco	1,029	1,102	1,808
Hydrocarbon oils	856	1,434	1,941
Protective duties	182	268	659
Purchase tax	686	1,394	—
Value added tax and car tax	—	—	4,206
Betting and gaming	43	151	285
Other	146	22	14
Total	3,617	5,349	10,802
Motor vehicle licence duties	270	468	820
Selective employment tax	141	666	—
Miscellaneous taxes on expenditure	121	244	550
less Export rebates	−96	−5	−7
less Bus fuel rebates	−6	−21	−45
Total taxes on expenditure	4,047	6,701	12,120
National insurance contributions	1,620	2,547	7,706
National health contributions	166	236	605
Redundancy fund contributions	18	52	115
Trading surpluses, rent, interest and dividends, etc.	766	1,475	3,286
Total	11,183	18,895	42,556

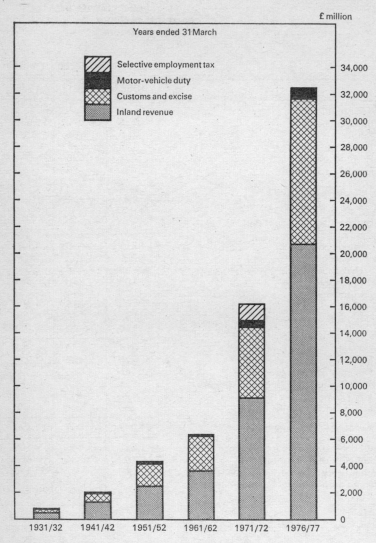

£ million

Years ended 31 March

Selective employment tax
Motor-vehicle duty
Customs and excise
Inland revenue

34,000
32,000
30,000
28,000
26,000
24,000
22,000
20,000
18,000
16,000
14,000
12,000
10,000
8,000
6,000
4,000
2,000
0

1931/32   1941/42   1951/52   1961/62   1971/72   1976/77

Chart 31 : Taxation
United Kingdom

Table 159

**Government[1] receipts
and expenditure
United Kingdom**

£ million

	1966	1971	1976
Taxes on income	4,566	7,884	18,724
Taxes on expenditure[2]	5,421	8,787	16,660
National insurance, etc. contributions	1,804	2,835	8,426
Trading income, rent, interest, etc.	1,312	2,254	5,314
Taxes on capital	315	663	885
Total receipts[3]	13,418	22,423	50,009
Goods and services	8,206	12,825	31,983
Current and capital transfers	5,212	9,598	18,026
Total[3]	13,418	22,423	50,009
Financial assets (net lending, etc.)	1,030	776	8,497
Total expenditure[4]	14,448	23,199	58,506

1. General government, i.e. central government and local authorities combined.
2. Central government taxes and local rates.
3. Current and capital account, excluding financial transactions.
4. A functional analysis is shown in Table 161.

Table 160

**Financial transactions of the
public sector**

£ million

	1966	1971	1976
Financial deficit[1] : general government	6	−677	5,918
public corporations	848	1,098	2,411
Public sector net lending, etc.	226	378	1,457
Total	1,080	799	9,786
Miscellaneous financial transactions (net receipts)	119	−574	274
Public sector borrowing requirement	961	1,373	9,512
Total	1,080	799	9,786

1. The excess of current and capital expenditure over receipts.

Table 161

Government expenditure[1]
United Kingdom

£ million

	1966	1971	1976
Military defence	2,202	2,760	6,176
Civil defence	19	7	29
External relations	281	385	1,045
Roads and public lighting	471	839	1,625
Transport and communication	373	555	1,141
Employment services	71	177	689
Other industry and trade	795	1,824	2,777
Research	151	232	483
Agriculture, forestry, fishing and food	307	497	1,199
Housing and environmental services	1,550	2,295	7,248
of which:			
Housing	*979*	*1,307*	*5,190*
Water, sewerage and refuse disposal	*255*	*470*	*646*
Public health services	*40*	*63*	*159*
Land drainage and coast protection	*20*	*35*	*73*
Parks, pleasure grounds, etc.	*71*	*130*	*412*
Miscellaneous local government services	*185*	*290*	*768*
Libraries, museums and arts	60	112	329
Police	241	439	1,137
Prisons	34	76	234
Parliament and law courts	43	100	333
Fire service	55	96	265
Social services	5,904	9,924	26,337
of which:			
Education	*1,700*	*2,899*	*7,340*
National health service	*1,375*	*2,248*	*6,182*
Personal social services	*111*	*310*	*1,128*
School meals, milk and welfare foods	*141*	*159*	*454*
Social security benefits	*2,577*	*4,308*	*11,233*
Finance and tax collection	180	323	768
Other services (include war-damage and records, etc.)	52	160	425
Debt interest	1,465	2,089	5,446
Non-trading capital consumption	194	309	820
Total government expenditure	14,448	23,199	58,506

1. Government expenditure is the current, capital and financial expenditure of central and local government excluding amounts transferred between the two sub-sectors.

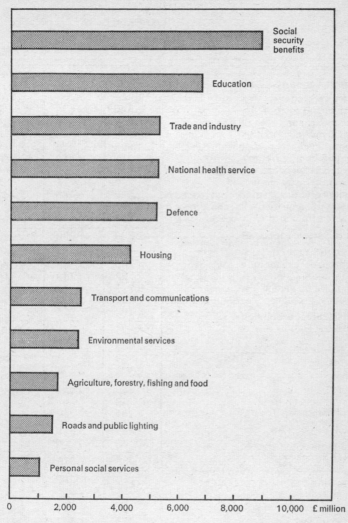

**Chart 32: Major items of
government expenditure, 1975
United Kingdom**

Table 162

Income and expenditure of
the personal sector
United Kingdom

£ million

	1976	1971	1966
Current account			
Income before tax			
Wages and salaries	20,389	29,673	67,185
Pay in cash and kind of HM Forces	523	758	1,473
Employers' contributions to national insurance, etc. and pension funds	1,902	3,228	9,981
Income from self-employment[1]	2,671	4,383	10,208
Rent, dividends and net interest	3,830	5,022	10,451
Current transfers to charities	30	38	42
Current grants from general government	2,825	4,783	12,822
Imputed charge for capital consumption of private non-profitmaking bodies	39	68	192
Total personal income[1]	32,209	47,953	112,354
Expenditure			
Consumers' expenditure	24,260	35,399	73,656
Net transfers abroad	22	13	65
UK taxes on income: accruals	3,727	6,515	18,049
National insurance, etc. contributions	1,804	2,835	8,426
Total current expenditure	29,813	44,762	100,196
Balance[2]	2,396	3,191	12,158
Total	32,209	47,953	112,354
Capital account			
Receipts			
Saving[2]	2,396	3,191	12,158
Additions to tax reserves	38	91	439
Capital transfers (net)	161	249	703
Total	2,595	3,531	13,300
Expenditure			
Dwellings[3]	698	1,060	2,286
Purchases *less* sales of land and existing buildings	−127	134	−149
Other fixed capital formation	505	705	1,409
Increase in value of stocks, etc.	64	273	869
Taxes on capital	313	568	737
Capital transfers to public corporations	4	7	26
Net acquisition of financial assets	1,138	784	8,122
Total	2,595	3,531	13,300

1. Before providing for depreciation and stock appreciation.
2. Saving before providing for depreciation and stock appreciation but after providing for additions to tax reserves.   3. Excluding existing dwellings and land.

Table 163

**Real personal disposable income
United Kingdom**

At 1970 prices

1970 = 100

	Total population	Real personal disposable income	Real personal disposable income per head
1951	91·1	56·8	62.4
1952	91·4	57·6	63·0
1953	91·6	60·5	66·0
1954	92·0	62·5	67·9
1955	92·3	65·4	70·9
1956	92·6	67·1	72·4
1957	93·0	68·2	73·3
1958	93·4	69·4	74·3
1959	93·9	73·0	77·7
1960	94·7	77·8	82·2
1961	95·4	81·0	84·9
1962	96·2	81·6	84·8
1963	96·7	85·3	88·2
1964	97·3	88·4	90·9
1965	97·9	90·7	92·6
1966	98·4	92·6	94·1
1967	98·9	94·0	95·0
1968	99·3	95·7	96·3
1969	99·7	96·5	96·7
1970	100·0	100·0	100·0
1971	100·3	102·7	102·3
1972	100·6	111·0	110·3
1973	100·9	117·5	116·4
1974	101·0	119·2	118·1
1975	100·9	119·7	118·6
1976	100·9	119·2	118·2

Table 164

**Income tax rates and allowances
United Kingdom**

	1976/77	1977/78
Personal allowance	£	£
Single person	735	845
Wife's earned income	735	845
Married man	1,085	1,295
Child[1] – under 11	300	300
11–16	335	335
over 16	365	365
Age allowance – single	1,010	1,120
married	1,555	1,765
Additional relief for children	350	450
Dependent relative		
Single woman claimant	145	145
Others	100	100
Housekeeper	100	100
Relative taking charge of younger brother or sister	100	100
Daughter's services	55	55
Blind person	180	180

Rates of personal taxation

Taxable income 1976/77	%	Taxable income 1977/78	%
Up to £5,000	35	Up to £6,000	34
Excess over £5,000		Excess over £6,000	
£5,000–5,500	40	£6,000–7,000	40
£5,500–6,500	45	£7,000–8,000	45
£6,500–7,500	50	£8,000–9,000	50
£7,500–8,500	55	£9,000–10,000	55
£8,500–10,000	60	£10,000–12,000	60
£10,000–12,000	65	£12,000–14,000	65
£12,000–15,000	70	£14,000–16,000	70
£15,000–20,000	75	£16,000–21,000	75
over £20,000	83	over £21,000	83
Surcharge on investment income		Surcharge on investment income	
Up to £1,000[2]	—	Up to £1,500[2]	—
£1,000–2,000[3]	10	£1,500–2,000[3]	10
Over £2,000	15	Over £2,000	15

1. The allowances for 1976/77 were reduced by £52 for each child for whom a full year's family allowance was received. For 1977/78 the child tax allowance is reduced by £104 for the first child and by £130 for the second and each subsequent child for whom a full year's child benefit is received. Unlike family allowances, the child benefit itself is not taxable.

2. £1,500 and £2,000 respectively in the case of the elderly.

3. £1,500, £2,000, and £2,000–2,500 respectively in the case of the elderly.

Table 165

**Distribution of tax units
by income before tax
United Kingdom**

Inland Revenue Annual Survey

Year ended 5 April

Lower limit of range of income	1974/75 Annual Survey			
	Number of tax units	Income before tax	Taxes on income	Income after tax
	Thousands	£ million		
Total incomes	28,274	64,675	11,847	52,828
Income before tax £				
Under 625	2,073	1,122	—	1,122
625	1,591	1,145	6	1,139
750	2,919	2,593	54	2,539
1,000	2,682	3,027	186	2,841
1,250	1,976	2,719	265	2,454
1,500	1,663	2,705	364	2,341
1,750	1,807	3,381	520	2,861
2,000	3,452	7,730	1,258	6,472
2,500	3,067	8,409	1,460	6,949
3,000	3,966	13,635	2,536	11,099
4,000	1,681	7,432	1,598	5,834
5,000	623	3,374	801	2,573
6,000	435	2,953	786	2,167
8,000	148	1,313	420	893
10,000	66	719	270	449
12,000	53	708	311	397
15,000	39	650	308	342
20,000 and over	33	1,060	704	356

Table 166

**Distribution of tax units
by income after tax
United Kingdom**

Inland Revenue Annual Survey
Year ended 5 April

Lower limit of range of income	1974/75 Annual Survey			
	Number of tax units	Income before tax	Taxes on income	Income after tax
	Thousands	£ million		
Total incomes	28,274	64,675	11,847	52,828
Income after tax £				
Under 625	2,077	1,119	4	1,115
625	1,706	1,241	15	1,226
750	3,489	3,246	154	3,092
1,000	3,304	4,093	370	3,723
1,250	2,506	4,004	557	3,447
1,500	2,322	4,519	740	3,779
1,750	2,126	4,775	793	3,982
2,000	3,874	10,469	1,789	8,680
2,500	2,865	9,537	1,704	7,833
3,000	2,806	11,971	2,443	9,528
4,000	658	3,852	947	2,905
5,000	285	2,179	641	1,538
6,000	177	1,979	775	1,204
8,000	55	948	461	487
10,000	16	394	222	172
12,000	5	181	112	69
15,000	2	99	67	32
20,000 and over	1	69	53	16

Table 167

Percentage shares of income, before and after tax, received by given quantile groups in 1972/73, 1973/74 and 1974/75
United Kingdom

percentage

Quantile group		Before tax			After tax		
		1972/73	1973/74	1974/75	1972/73	1973/74	1974/75
Top 1	per cent	6·4	6·5	6·2	4·4	4·5	4·0
2– 5	„ „	10·8	10·6	10·6	9·8	9·8	9·7
6–10	„ „	9·7	9·7	9·8	9·4	9·3	9·5
Top 10 per cent		26·9	26·8	26·6	23·6	23·6	23·2
11– 20	„ „	15·8	15·6	15·8	15·8	15·5	15·8
21– 30	„ „	13·1	12·9	13·1	13·2	13·2	13·2
31– 40	„ „	11·0	11·2	11·0	11·2	11·2	11·4
41– 50	„ „	9·2	9·3	9·3	9·5	9·5	9·4
51– 60	„ „	7·5	7·5	7·6	8·0	7·8	7·8
61– 70	„ „	5·9	5·8	5·8	6·5	6·4	6·4
71– 80	„ „	4·8	4·7	4·6	5·5	5·4	5·3
81– 90	„ „	}5·9	3·5	3·6	}6·9	4·2	4·4
91–100	„ „		2·7	2·6		3·2	3·1
Median : £ per year		1,338	1,550	1,913	1,187	1,348	1,604
Mean : £ per year		1,614	1,857	2,287	1,382	1,571	1,868

Table 168

Average household income by household composition[1] United Kingdom

£ per year

Code[2] Household composition	1966		1971		1975	
	A	B	A	B	A	B
1 Adult – non-pensioner	623	620	907	888	1,724	1,699
1 Adult – pensioner[3]	19	288	30	421	52	846
2 Adults – non-pensioner	1,233	1,133	1,847	1,642	3,594	3,096
2 Adults – pensioner	45	456	55	638	133	1,314
2 Adults 1 child	1,392	1,233	1,982	1,727	3,880	3,176
2 Adults 2 children	1,467	1,312	2,108	1,879	4,039	3,345
2 Adults 3 children	1,387	1,318	2,047	1,891	4,266	3,539
2 Adults 4 children	1,265	1,246	2,097	2,005	3,594	3,374
3 Adults	1,715	1,562	2,504	2,237	4,896	4,132
3 Adults 1 child	1,890	1,676	2,761	2,402	5,186	4,316
3 Adults 2 children	1,568	1,509	2,744	2,491	5,089	4,430
4 Adults	2,350	2,091	3,582	3,070	6,989	5,625
All households in the sample	1,301	1,222	1,802	1,671	3,386	3,016

1. Source: Family Expenditure Survey.
2. Code: A Original income
        B Disposable income.
3. A pensioner household is one which derives at least three-quarters of its income from national insurance retirement and similar pensions and/or benefits paid in supplementation.

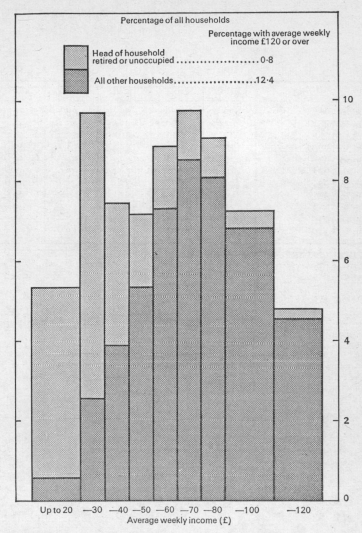

*Chart 33: Households in
selected income groups
United Kingdom
1975*

Table 169

Internal purchasing power of the pound[1]
United Kingdom

pence

	1966	1971	1974	1975	1976
100p in 1966	100	76	56	45	$38\frac{1}{2}$
100p in 1967	$102\frac{1}{2}$	78	$57\frac{1}{2}$	46	$39\frac{1}{2}$
100p in 1968	$107\frac{1}{2}$	$81\frac{1}{2}$	60	$48\frac{1}{2}$	$41\frac{1}{2}$
100p in 1969	113	86	$63\frac{1}{2}$	51	$43\frac{1}{2}$
100p in 1970	$120\frac{1}{2}$	$91\frac{1}{2}$	$67\frac{1}{2}$	54	$46\frac{1}{2}$
100p in 1971	132	100	$73\frac{1}{2}$	$59\frac{1}{2}$	51
100p in 1972	141	107	79	63	$54\frac{1}{2}$
100p in 1973	154	117	86	$69\frac{1}{2}$	$59\frac{1}{2}$
100p in 1974	$178\frac{1}{2}$	$135\frac{1}{2}$	100	$80\frac{1}{2}$	69
100p in 1975	222	$168\frac{1}{2}$	124	100	86
100p in 1976	259	$196\frac{1}{2}$	145	$116\frac{1}{2}$	100

1. Based on changes in the General Index of Retail Prices.

Table 170

General index of retail prices
United Kingdom

	1966[1]	1971[1]	1974[2]	1975[2]	1976[2]
All items	116·5	153·4	108·5	134·8	157·1
Food	115·6	155·6	106·1	133·3	159·9
Alcoholic drink	121·7	152·7	109·7	135·2	159·3
Tobacco	120·8	138·5	115·9	147·7	171·3
Housing	128·5	172·6	105·8	125·5	143·2
Fuel and light	120·9	160·9	110·7	147·4	182·4
Durable household goods	107·2	135·4	107·9	131·2	144·2
Clothing and footwear	109·9	132·2	109·4	125·7	139·4
Transport and vehicles	109·9	147·2	111·0	143·9	166·0
Miscellaneous goods	112·5	159·1	111·2	138·6	161·3
Services	120·5	169·6	106·8	135·5	159·5
Meals bought and consumed outside the home	116·1	165·0	108·2	132·4	157·3

The index measures the changes in the average level of retail prices of the commodities and services purchased by nearly nine-tenths of households in the United Kingdom, including practically all wage earners and most small and medium salary earners.

1. Based on 16 January 1962 = 100.

2. Based on 15 January 1974 = 100. The 'All items' figure at 15 January 1974 is 191·8 on the old basis.

Table 171
**Consumers' expenditure
United Kingdom**

£ million

	1976	1971	1966
Current prices			
Food (household expenditure)	5,297	6,924	14,095
Alcoholic drink	1,626	2,593	5,912
Tobacco	1,504	1,691	3,106
Housing	2,851	4,612	10,921
Fuel and light	1,161	1,619	3,595
Clothing and footwear	2,154	2,990	5,938
Durable goods	1,757	3,089	5,764
Other household goods	732	1,031	2,061
Books, newspapers, magazines	349	541	1,089
Chemists' goods	345	581	1,245
Miscellaneous recreational goods	507	846	1,736
Other miscellaneous goods	318	455	1,025
Running costs of motor vehicles	1,083	1,849	4,418
Travel	801	1,161	2,467
Communication services	215	395	1,192
Entertainment and recreational services	425	620	1,370
Catering (meals and accommodation)	1,250	1,697	3,266
Insurance	292	540	1,142
Other items	1,451	2,184	3,974
less Expenditure by foreign tourists, etc. in the United Kingdom	−279	−588	−1,936
Consumers' expenditure abroad	421	569	1,276
Total expenditure at current prices	24,260	35,399	73,656
Total expenditure at 1970 prices	29,280	32,675	35,405

	1971 over 1966	1976 over 1971
Percentage increase		
in value (current prices)	45·9	108·1
in volume (1970 prices)	11·6	8·4
in prices	30·8	92·0

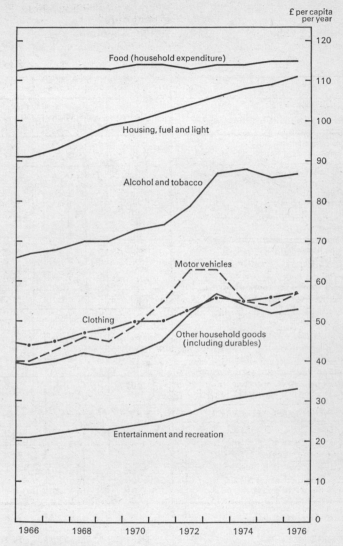

£ per capita
per year

Food (household expenditure)

Housing, fuel and light

Alcohol and tobacco

Motor vehicles

Clothing

Other household goods
(including durables)

Entertainment and recreation

1966 1968 1970 1972 1974 1976

Chart 34: Consumers'
expenditure: selected items
at 1970 prices
United Kingdom

Table 172

Average weekly household expenditure[1]
United Kingdom

Family Expenditure Survey 1976

	Composition of household		
	One adult	One adult with children	One man and one woman
Number of persons per household	1·00	2·98	2·00
Persons working per household	0·38	0·69	1·14
Average weekly household expenditure	Percentages		
Housing	22·6	19·1	15·9
Fuel, light and power	7·9	7·3	6·0
Food	23·1	28·7	23·8
Alcoholic drink[2]	4·5	1·9	5·1
Tobacco[2]	2·9	3·0	3·7
Clothing and footwear	5·5	8·9	6·8
Durable household goods	4·6	6·2	7·3
Other goods	6·6	7·3	7·3
Transport and vehicles	10·2	7·9	13·1
Services and miscellaneous	12·1	9·7	11·0
Total expenditure (100%) £	29·59	46·16	57·08

	Composition of household		
	One man, one woman and one child	One man, one woman and two children	One man, one woman and three children
Number of persons per household	3·00	4·00	5·00
Persons working per household	1·64	1·64	1·78
Average weekly household expenditure	Percentages		
Housing	15·0	14·8	13·4
Fuel, light and power	5·6	5·5	5·2
Food	24·3	25·8	27·6
Alcoholic drink[2]	4·7	4·1	3·9
Tobacco[2]	3·4	3·5	3·4
Clothing and footwear	8·0	8·3	9·2
Durable household goods	7·5	6·6	6·7
Other goods	7·6	7·5	7·2
Transport and vehicles	14·0	13·6	12·4
Service and miscellaneous	9·9	10·3	11·0
Total expenditure (100%) £	69·04	72·80	79·21

1. These figures are subject to sampling variations.
2. Expenditure on these items is known to be understated.

Table 173

Percentage of households with certain durable goods in the two-year period 1975–76[1] United Kingdom

Family Expenditure Survey

	Percentage in sample with		
	Telephone	Washing machine	Refrigerator
United Kingdom	52	72	87
North	39	84	81
Yorkshire and Humberside	48	83	85
East Midlands	46	81	85
East Anglia	49	75	90
South East except Greater London	63	69	94
Greater London	65	55	92
South West	51	67	92
West Midlands	48	74	82
North West	52	70	83
Wales	39	77	85
Scotland	52	78	82

	% in sample with		
	One or more cars	Full or partial central heating	Number of households in sample
United Kingdom	56	47	14,406
North	51	52	919
Yorkshire and Humberside	51	42	1,375
East Midlands	57	50	968
East Anglia	71	55	522
South East except Greater London	67	57	2,532
Greater London	51	42	1,691
South West	67	53	1,078
West Midlands	58	45	1,303
North West	48	41	1,618
Wales	58	40	726
Scotland	45	43	1,377

1. These figures are subject to sampling variations.

Table 174

Distribution of wealth[1] among identified wealth owners Great Britain

		1966		1971		1974	
		No. of cases (000's)	£ thousand million	No. of cases (000's)	£ thousand million	No. of cases (000's)	£ thousand million
Ranges of net wealth							
Over £	Not over £						
	1,000	6,335	3·5	4,211	2.1	3,410	2·0
1,000	3,000	5,573	10·3	5,491	10·1	4,775	8·6
3,000	5,000	2,739	10·6	2,912	11·4	2,223	8·7
Total not over	5,000	14,647	24·4	12,614	23·6	10,408	19·3
5,000	10,000	1,944	13·6	3,799	27·1	4,131	30·3
10,000	15,000	539	6·8	962	11·8	2,166	26·5
15,000	20,000	251	4·4	412	6·6	757	13·3
20,000	25,000	146	3·2	232	5·2	415	9·6
25,000	50,000	251	8·6	380	13·0	640	21·7
50,000	100,000	99	6·7	158	10·3	229	15·4
100,000	200,000	30	4·0	49	6·7	65	9·2
200,000		14	5·1	26	8·4	26	11·8
Total under £10,000		16,591	38·0	16,413	50·7	14,539	49·6
Total over £10,000		1,330	38·8	2,219	62·0	4,298	107·4
Total		17,921	76·8	18,632	112·7	18,837	157·1
Total number as a percentage of home population aged 15 and over		*43·9*		*46·0*		*45·3*	

1. The estimates are derived from estate duty statistics and are thought to cover about 80 per cent of all wealth held by or on behalf of individuals.

Table 175

Net acquisition of financial assets

£ million

	1966	1971	1976
Central government	891	1,832	−4,254
Local authorities	−897	−1,155	−1,664
General government	−6	677	−5,918
Public corporations	−848	−1,098	−2,411
Public sector	−854	−421	−8,329
Financial companies and institutions	−73	−283	−1,078
Industrial and commercial companies	−270	710	−1,102
Personal sector	1,138	784	8,122
Overseas sector[1]	−104	−1,058	1,405
Residual error[2]	163	268	982

1. Equals, apart from the change in the sign, the current balance in the balance of payments accounts, *plus* capital transfers.
2. The residual error in the national income accounts.

Table 176

**Changes in money stock and
domestic credit expansion
United Kingdom**

£ million

	1966	1971	1976
Notes and coin in circulation with public	66	273	811
Private sector sterling sight deposits	−63	782	1,175
Money stock M₁[1]	3	1,055	1,986
Private sector time deposits	430	1,361	1,582
Public sector deposits	13	39	−3
Sterling money stock M₃[2]	446	2,455	3,565
UK residents' deposits in other currencies	33	−89	986
Money stock M₃[3]	479	2,366	4,551
Public sector borrowing requirement	961	1,373	9,512
Net acquisition of public sector debt by the non-bank private sector	262	2,106	6,089
Sterling lending to the private sector	34	1,627	3,431
Bank lending in sterling to overseas	−22	296	650
Domestic credit expansion [4,5]	711	1,190	7,504
External and foreign currency finance	149	−1,633	3,115
Non-deposit liabilities (net)	116	368	824
Money stock sterling M₃	446	2,455	3,565

1. M_1 equals lines 1 + 2.
2. Sterling money stock M_3 equals lines 3 + 4 + 5.
3. M_3 equals lines 6 + 7.
4. Domestic credit expansion equals lines 9 − 10 + 11 + 12.
5. The authorities announced objectives for DCE on an old definition before the second quarter of 1971, but the figures for 1966 and 1971 have been recalculated on the new definition in order to facilitate comparison.

Note: Three definitions of money stock are shown in this table. The first definition (M_1) is a narrow one consisting of notes and coin in circulation with the public *plus* sterling sight deposits held by the private sector only. The second definition (M_3) comprises notes and coin in circulation with the public, together with all sterling deposits (including certificates of deposit) held by UK residents in both the public and the private sectors. The third definition equals sterling M_3 *plus* all deposits held by UK residents in other currencies.

Table 177

Analysis of bank advances[1]
United Kingdom[2]

£ million

	1967	1971	1976
Total[3]	7,536	16,030	32,213
Manufacturing industries:			
Food, drink and tobacco	268	414	1,209
Chemicals and allied industries	216	317	1,192
Metal manufacture	189	175	475
Electrical engineering	247	415	574
Other engineering and metal goods	480	891	1,345
Shipbuilding	76	329	442
Vehicles	278	463	451
Textiles, leather and clothing	237	313	653
Other manufacturing	313	496	1,255
Other production:			
Agriculture, forestry and fishing	492	556	1,068
Mining and quarrying	84	129	1,062
Construction	360	509	1,560
Financial:			
Hire-purchase finance companies	118	143	480
Property companies	337	430	2,848
Other financial	322	753	3,537
Services:			
Transport and communication	161	278	1,430
Public utilities and national government	67	146	2,303
Local government	96	72	540
Retail distribution	354	373	1,157
Other distribution	368	560	2,071
Professional, scientific and miscellaneous	479	671	2,387
Personal:			
House purchase	337	447	1,336
Other personal	545	746	2,832
Overseas residents	1,112	6,409	..

1. The annual figures are averages of February, May, August and November.
2. Great Britain in 1967 and 1971.
3. Because of difficulties of classification it is not possible to include advances before 1974 made by the six finance houses recognized or confirmed as banks in January 1972 or January 1973.

Table 178
Building societies[1]
Great Britain

	1966	1971	1976
Societies on register (number)	576	467	364
Share investors (thousands)	6,564	11,568	19,991
Depositors (thousands)	588	655	712
Borrowers (thousands)	2,992	3,896	4,609
Liabilities and provisions (£ million) :			
Total	6,044	12,427	27,204
Shares	5,596	11,695	25,760
Deposits	299	491	848
HM government advances	69	38	19
Other	81	203	578
Reserves and unappropriated surplus (£ million)	262	492	999
Assets (£ million) :			
Total	6,306	12,919	28,202
Mortgages	5,219	10,332	22,565
Investments	906	2,216	4,339
Cash	113	228	908
Other	69	144	391
Percentage rate of interest[2]			
Paid on shares	4·01	4·93	7·02
Paid on deposits	3·62	4·39	6·53
Received on mortgage advances	6·95	8·59	11·06

1. The figures for each year relate to accounting years ending on any date between 1 February of that year and 31 January of the following year.
2. Based on the mean of the amounts outstanding at the end of the previous and the current year.

Table 179

**Insurance companies established
in Great Britain**

Life assurance, motor vehicle, fire,
marine, aviation, etc. insurance
business

£ million

	1966	1971[1]	1974[1]
Life assurance, ordinary business[2]			
Income: premiums and consideration for			
annuities	928	1,705	2,622
other	411	1,077	1,432
Expenditure: claims paid and outstanding[3]	545	979	1,654
other	161	511	3,267
Life and annuity funds at end of year	7,315	12,046	14,880
Life assurance, industrial business			
Income: premiums	214	267	330
other	119	187	206
Expenditure: claims paid and outstanding[3]	159	221	259
other	97	126	389
Industrial assurance funds at end of year	1,640	2,083	2,187
Motor vehicle insurance business			
Income: premiums	501	636	938
other	12	30	57
Expenditure: claims paid and outstanding	340	389	586
other	164	192	295
Funds at end of year	211	649	1,066
Marine, aviation and transport business			
Income: premiums	114	243	337
other	10	6	22
Expenditure: claims	108	159	249
other	15	39	73
Funds at end of year	134	281	403

1. Figures for 1971 and 1974 are not completely comparable with 1966 as a
result of a change in reporting requirements.
2. Figures refer to companies established in the United Kingdom.
3. Including surrenders, annuities and cash bonuses.

Table 180

**Net acquisition from investment
of superannuation funds[1]
United Kingdom**

£ million

	1966	1971	1976
Total investment	533	876	3,132
Short-term assets (net):			
Cash in hand	12	−19	12
Local authority temporary debt	−6	−19	−44
Other	9	−26	22
British government securities	37	296	1,171
Local authority securities	1	−64	98
Overseas government provincial and municipal securities	−6	−5	−10
Company securities	351	509	1,118
Loans and mortgages	86	70	231
Land, property and ground rents	48	91	513
Property unit trusts	..	38	54
Other investments	1	5	7
Long-term borrowing[2]	..	—	−40

1. The table includes funded schemes of local authorities, public corporations and private-sector pension funds.
2. Positive items represent a decrease and negative items an increase in borrowing.

Table 181

National savings: net receipts and amounts remaining invested United Kingdom

	Year ended 31 December		£ million
	1966	1971	1976
Net receipts			
Total[1]	−248	325	363
National savings certificates	−129	32	153
Save As You Earn	—	30	53
National Savings Bank:			
Ordinary account	−126	39	−49
Investment account	53	45	−6
Trustee savings banks:			
Ordinary departments	−17	48	39
New department	62	74	−12
Premium savings bonds	45	92	76
British savings bonds[2]	−142	25	6
National savings stamps and gift tokens	..	..	−14
Amounts remaining invested (at end of period)			
Total[3]	8,335	9,220	12,350
National savings certificates:			
Principal	1,982	2,068	2,356
Accrued interest (estimated)	587	540	622
Save As You Earn:			
Principal	—	53	259
Accrued interest	—	1	31
National Savings Bank: [3]			
Ordinary account	1,740	1,455	1,534
Investment account	54	376	665
Trustee savings banks: [3]			
Ordinary departments	1,041	1,155	1,601
New department	1,110	1,642	2,616
Premium savings bonds	575	890	1,186
British savings bonds[2]	1,064	797	797
National savings stamps and gift tokens	..	..	32
Other securities on the National Savings Registers[4]	183	246	651

1. Including securities on the National Savings register.
2. Including Defence bonds and National development bonds.
3. Including accrued interest.
4. Nominal value held (National and Trustee savings banks sections).

Table 182

Short-term money rates
United Kingdom

per cent per annum

	Bank of England's minimum lending rate to the market[1]	Treasury bills		Deposits with local authorities	
		Average discount rate[2]	Yield[3]	7 days' notice	3 months' notice[4]
Last Friday of:					
1966	7	6·53	6·64	$7\frac{3}{8}$	$7\frac{1}{4}-7\frac{3}{16}$
1967	8	7·48	7·62	$8\frac{3}{8}-8\frac{1}{2}$	$7\frac{3}{4}-7\frac{7}{8}$
1968	7	6·78	6·90	$7\frac{1}{4}$	$7\frac{3}{4}$
1969	8	7·65	7·80	$8\frac{7}{8}$	$9-9\frac{1}{16}$
1970	7	6·82	6·93	$6\frac{3}{4}-6\frac{7}{8}$	$7\frac{1}{4}$
1971	5	4·41	4·46	$4\frac{1}{4}-4\frac{3}{8}$	$4\frac{1}{2}-4\frac{5}{8}$
1972	9	8·31	7·91	$8-8\frac{1}{8}$	$8\frac{3}{4}$
1973	13	12·42	12·82	$15\frac{1}{2}-16$	$16-16\frac{1}{8}$
1974	$11\frac{1}{2}$	10·99	11·30	$11-11\frac{1}{4}$	$13\frac{1}{4}$
1975	$11\frac{1}{2}$	10·77	10·93	$11\frac{3}{8}-11\frac{1}{2}$	$11\frac{1}{4}-11\frac{3}{8}$
1976	$14\frac{1}{4}$	13·51	13·98	$14\frac{7}{8}-15\frac{3}{8}$	$14\frac{3}{4}-15$
1976					
Jan.	10	9·30	9·52	$10\frac{1}{8}-10\frac{1}{4}$	$9\frac{7}{8}-9\frac{15}{16}$
Feb.	$9\frac{1}{4}$	8·62	8·80	$8\frac{7}{8}-9\frac{1}{8}$	$9-9\frac{1}{8}$
Mar.	9	8·42	8·60	$8\frac{1}{4}$	$8\frac{5}{8}-8\frac{3}{4}$
Apr.	$10\frac{1}{2}$	9·94	10·20	$9\frac{7}{8}$	$10\frac{1}{8}-10\frac{1}{4}$
May	$11\frac{1}{2}$	11·00	11·31	$10\frac{1}{2}-10\frac{3}{8}$	$11\frac{1}{4}-11\frac{3}{8}$
June	$11\frac{1}{2}$	10·99	11·30	$11-11\frac{1}{4}$	$11\frac{1}{8}-11\frac{1}{4}$
July	$11\frac{1}{2}$	10·87	11·17	$11-11\frac{1}{8}$	$11\frac{1}{16}-11\frac{1}{4}$
Aug.	$11\frac{1}{2}$	10·94	11·25	$10\frac{5}{8}-10\frac{3}{4}$	$11\frac{1}{8}-11\frac{1}{4}$
Sept.	13	12·35	12·74	$12\frac{5}{8}-12\frac{3}{4}$	$12\frac{3}{4}-12\frac{7}{8}$
Oct.	15	14·43	14·97	$15-15\frac{1}{4}$	$15\frac{1}{4}-15\frac{1}{2}$
Nov.	$14\frac{3}{4}$	14·03	14·54	$15\frac{1}{2}$	$15-15\frac{1}{4}$
Dec.	$14\frac{1}{4}$	13·51	13·98	$14\frac{7}{8}-15\frac{3}{8}$	$14\frac{3}{4}-15$

1. Bank rate until 12 October 1972. With effect from 13 October, the Bank's minimum lending rate to the market will normally be $\frac{1}{2}$% higher than the average rate of discount for Treasury Bills established at the weekly tender, rounded to the nearest $\frac{1}{4}$% above; the rate normally becomes effective for Bank lending from the following Monday.

2. Average rate of discount on allotment for 91 day bills at the weekly tender.

3. Average discount rate expressed as the rate at which interest is earned during the life of the bills.

4. For a minimum term of 3 months and thereafter at 7 days' notice.

Table 183

Security yields and prices
United Kingdom

	1966	1971	1976
British government securities			
Gross redemption yields:[1]			
Short-dated (5 years)	6·77	6·68	12·06
Medium-dated (10 years)	6·87	8·24	13·61
Long-dated (20 years)	6·94	8·90	14·43
$2\frac{1}{2}$% Consols[2]			
Net price	36·7	27·6	17·6
Gross flat yield	6·80	9·05	14·25
Company securities[3]			
Ordinary industrial shares			
Price index (10 April 1962=100)	107·59	168·07	162·91
Dividend yield	5·67	3·96	6·16
Preference stocks			
Price index (10 April 1962=100)	100·12	76·00	65·46
Yield average	7·15	10·23	14·48
Debenture and loan stocks			
Price index (10 April 1962=100)	92·62	73·66	48·68
Redemption yield	7·70	10·55	15·19

1. There was a break in the series in 1970 due to a change in method of calculation.
2. Excluding gross accrued interest; tax is ignored.
3. The series are calculated from the FT–Actuaries share indices.

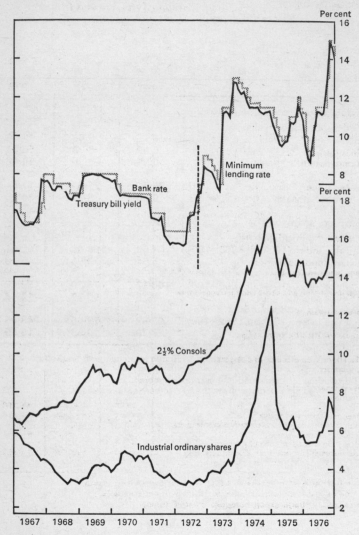

Per cent

Minimum
lending rate

Per cent

Bank rate

Treasury bill yield

2½% Consols

Industrial ordinary shares

**Chart 35: Interest rates and
yields
United Kingdom**

Table 184

**Balance of payments
United Kingdom**

£ million

	1966	1971	1976
Current account			
Exports	5,276	9,061	25,416
Imports	5,342	8,781	28,987
Visible balance	−66	+280	−3,571
Invisible balance	+170	+778	+2,166
Current balance	+104	+1,058	−1,405
Investment and other capital transactions[1]			
Official long-term capital	−81	−274	−158
Overseas investment in UK public sector	+35	+107	+203
Overseas investment in UK private sector	+264	+1,052	+2,051
UK private investment overseas	−303	−836	−2,100
Overseas currency borrowing or lending (net) by UK banks[2]	−192	+471	−106
Changes in external sterling liabilities	−101	+1,422	−1,152
Trade credit and other short-term transactions[3]	−200	−126	−1,552
Total investment and other capital transactions	−578	+1,816	−2,814
Balancing item	−73	+272	+591
Balance for official financing	−547	+3,146	+3,628
Allocation of Special Drawing Rights	—	+125	—
Gold subscription to IMF	−44	—	—
Official financing[1]			
Net transactions with:			
IMF	+15	−554	+1,018
Other monetary authorities	+294	−1,263	−34
Foreign currency borrowing by public sector under exchange cover scheme	—	+82	+1,791
Transfer from dollar portfolio to reserves	+316	—	—
Official reserves (drawings on +/additions to−)	−34	−1,536	+853

1. + indicates an increase in liabilities or a decrease in assets.
2. Includes borrowing to finance UK investment overseas.
3. Excluding trade credit between 'related' firms.

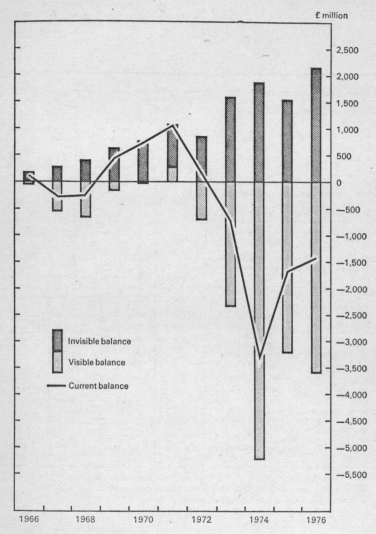

**Chart 36: Balance of
payments: current account
United Kingdom**

Table 185

Value of external trade in the balance of payments United Kingdom

£ million

	1966	1971	1976
Exports			
By areas:			
European Economic Community	1,356	2,512	9,025
Other Western Europe	862	1,519	3,990
North America	868	1,416	3,077
Other developed countries	714	1,077	1,940
Oil-exporting countries	297	580	3,168
Rest of the world	1,179	1,957	4,216
Total	5,276	9,061	25,416
By commodity:			
Food, beverages and tobacco	339	569	1,654
Basic materials	208	280	774
Mineral fuels and lubricants	134	236	1,254
Manufactured goods	4,403	7,715	20,910
Commodities and transactions not classified according to kind	192	261	824
Total	5,276	9,061	25,416
Imports			
By areas:			
European Economic Community	1,392	2,697	11,129
Other Western Europe	662	1,401	3,994
North America	1,094	1,587	3,894
Other developed countries	602	854	1,930
Oil-exporting countries	417	768	3,867
Rest of the world	1,175	1,474	4,173
Total	5,342	8,781	28,987
By commodity:			
Food, beverages and tobacco	1,553	1,966	4,627
Basic materials	894	1,047	2,792
Mineral fuels and lubricants	479	918	5,243
Manufactured goods	2,333	4,723	15,861
Commodities and transactions not classified according to kind	83	127	464
Total	5,342	8,781	28,987

Table 186

**Services and other invisible transactions
United Kingdom**

£ million

	1966	1971	1976
Credits			
Services			
General government	42	59	215
Private sector (and public corporations)			
Sea transport	765	1,621	3,251
Civil aviation	180	354	1,051
Travel	219	486	1,628
Financial services	125	435	1,086
Other services	530	865	2,190
Interest, profits and dividends			
General government	48	91	253
Private sector (and public corporations)	914	1,388	3,493
Transfers			
General government	—	—	251
Private sector	135	215	420
Total credits	2,958	5,514	13,838
Debits			
Services			
General government	332	374	969
Private sector (and public corporations)			
Sea transport	760	1,673	3,206
Civil aviation	149	297	810
Travel	297	439	1,008
Other services	338	546	1,584
Interest, profits and dividends			
General government	214	295	905
Private sector (and public corporations)	361	679	1,662
Transfers			
General government	180	205	1,043
Private sector	157	228	485
Total debits	2,788	4,736	11,672
Invisible balance	+170	+778	+2,166

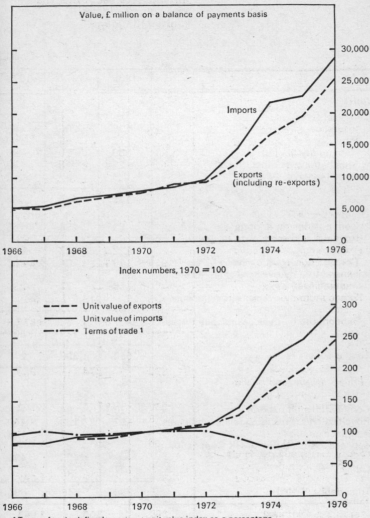

Value, £ million on a balance of payments basis

Imports

Exports
(including re-exports)

Index numbers, 1970 = 100

- - - - Unit value of exports
——— Unit value of imports
-·-·- Terms of trade [1]

[1] Terms of trade defined as export unit value index as a percentage
of import value index

**Chart 37: Imports and
exports of goods
United Kingdom**

Table 187

**Private services (other than transport and travel[1])
United Kingdom**

£ million

	1966	1971	1976
Credits			
Financial services:			
Insurance	39	236	458
Banking	22	59	169
Commodity trading	30	70	201
Merchanting of other goods	25	13	46
Brokerage, etc.	29	57	212
Total	125	435	1,086
Other services			
Commissions on imports	83	94	165
Royalties and services to related concerns	122	222	510
Construction work overseas	40	104	456
Expenditure by overseas students and journalists	46	71	235
Expenditure by overseas governments, etc.	47	77	265
Expenditure by overseas military forces	31	58	58
Other	161	239	501
Total credits	655	1,300	3,276
Debits			
Commissions on exports	70	94	178
Royalties and services to related concerns	97	183	440
Agency expenses	44	82	123
Services associated with UK Continental Shelf activities (net)	—	25	490
Other	127	162	353
Total debits	338	546	1,584

1. Shown in Table 186 as 'Financial services' and 'Other services'.

Table 188
Interest, profits and dividends
United Kingdom

£ million

	1966	1971	1976
Credits			
Direct investment[1]	429	718	2,064
Portfolio investment	153	166	234
Other[2]	380	595	1,448
Total credits	962	1,479	3,746
of which:			
Private sector (and public corporations)	914	1,388	3,493
General government	48	91	253
Debits			
Direct investment[1]	204	390	1,045
Portfolio investment	83	135	353
Other[2]	288	449	1,169
Total debits	575	974	2,567
of which:			
Private sector (and public corporations)	361	679	1,662
General government	214	295	905
Interest, profits and dividends (net)	+387	+505	+1,179
of which:			
Private sector (and public corporations)	+553	+709	+1,831
General government	−166	−204	−652

1. Department of Trade inquiry into overseas direct investment. Credits exclude the earnings of UK oil companies; debits exclude the earnings of UK oil and insurance companies.
2. Including oil companies.

Table 189

**Area population and population
growth
1975**

Mid-year estimates

	Population (millions)	Area in thousands sq. km	Population per sq. km	Percentage increase population 1961–1971
United Kingdom	56·04	244·0	230	5·3
Belgium	9·80	30·5	321	5·4
Denmark	5·06	43·1	117	8·7
France	52·75	547·0	96	11·0
Germany (FR) [1]	61·83	248·6	249	9·6
Irish Republic	3·13	70·3	44	7·1
Italy	55·83	301·3	185	8·4
Luxembourg	0·36	2·6	139	6·2
Netherlands	13·67	41·2	332	13·8
Japan	111·46	370·0	301	11·3
USA	213·61	9,363·1	23	12·6
USSR	254·38	22,402·0	11	12·3

1. Federal Republic of Germany and West Berlin.

Table 190

**Population by age and sex
1975**

	Total (thousands)		Percentage aged:		
	Male	Female	Under 15	15–64	65+
United Kingdom	27,328	28,756	23·5	62·6	13·9
Belgium	4,793	4,996	22·5	63·6	13·9
Denmark	2,504	2,550	22·6	64·1	13·3
France	25,819	26,857	24·1	62·6	13·3
Germany (FR)	29,604	32,387	21·8	63·9	14·3
Irish Republic	1,564	1,554	31·1	57·7	11·2
Italy	27,223	28,424	24·2	63·8	12·0
Luxembourg	177	181	20·1	66·8	13·1
Netherlands	6,771	6,828	25·6	63·7	10·7
Japan	55,115	56,819	24·3	67·8	7·9
USA[1]	102,945	108,446	25·8	63·9	10·3
USSR[1]	118,144	136,238	25·8	65·1	9·1

1. 1974 figures.

Table 191
Births and deaths
1975

	Crude birth rate per 1,000 population	Crude death rate per 1,000 population	Infant mortality per 1,000 live births[1]
United Kingdom	12·4	11·8	16·0
Belgium	12.2	12·2	14·6
Denmark	14·2	10·1	10·4
France	14·1	10·6	13·6
Germany (FR)	9·7	12·1	19·7
Irish Republic	21·6	10·7	18·4
Italy	14·8	9·9	20·9
Luxembourg	11·1	12·2	14·8
Netherlands	13·0	8·3	10·6
Japan	17·2	6·4	10·1
USA	14·7	9·0	16·1
USSR	18·2	9·3	27·7[1]

1. 1974.

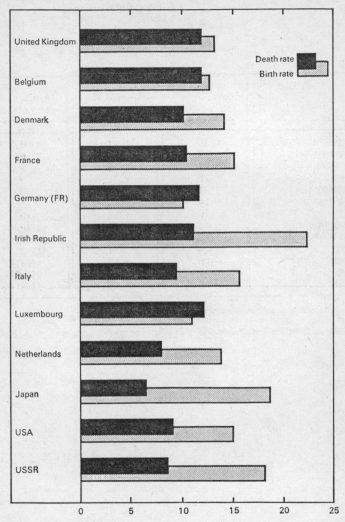

Chart 38: Birth and death rates per thousand population 1974

Table 192
Marriages
1975

	Minimum legal age[1]		Marriage rate per 1,000 population
	Males	Females	
United Kingdom	16	16	7·7
Belgium	18	15	7·4
Denmark	21	18	6·3
France	18	15	7·3
Germany (FR)	21	16	6·2
Irish Republic	14	12	6·8
Italy	16	14	6·7
Luxembourg	18	15	6·8
Netherlands	18	16	7·3
Japan	18	16	9·1[2]
USA	[3]	[3]	10·5[2]
USSR	18	18	10·1[2]

1. In most cases with written parental consent.
2. 1974.
3. Varies among major civil divisions or ethnic or religious groups.

Table 193

**Health services
1974**

	Population per doctor	Population per dentist	Population per hospital bed
England and Wales	760	3,460	110[4]
Scotland	620	3,100	80
Northern Ireland	730[4]	3,090[4]	90[4]
Belgium	570	4,550	110
Denmark	620[2]	1,310[2]	100[3]
France	680	2,090	100
Germany (FR)	520	1,960	90
Irish Republic	850[2]	4,570[2]	90
Italy	500[4]	..	90[2]
Luxembourg	930	3,030	90
Netherlands	670	3,290	100
Japan	870[4]	2,740[4]	80[2]
USA	610	1,970	150
USSR	340	2,480	90[4]

1. Government health establishments.
2. 1972.
3. 1970.
4. 1973.

Table 194
Housing

	Year	Average number of persons per household	Average number of rooms per dwelling	Percentage of occupied dwellings with:	
				flush WC	water piped inside housing unit
United Kingdom	1971	3·0	3·9	99·2[1]	92·9[1]
Belgium	1970	3·0	5·0	62·5	88·0
Denmark	1970	2·7	3·5	96·2	98·7
France	1975	2·9	3·6	51·8[2]	96·6
Germany (FR)	1972	2·7	4·2	94·2	99·2
Irish Republic	1971	3·9	4·7	70·0	73·2
Italy	1971	3·3	3·7	79·1	86·1
Luxembourg	1970	3·1	5·3	93·0	98·4
Netherlands	1971	3·2	5·2[3]	67·5[4]	96·9
Japan	1973	3·6	4·0[5]	31·4	98·3
USA	1970	3·1	5·1	96·0	97·5
USSR	1969	3·7	2·8[6]	··	··

1. Proportion of all households having sole or shared use of the amenity.
2. 1968.
3. 1960.
4. 1956.
5. Estimated.
6. 1965.

Table 195

**Motor vehicles in use
1975**

	Commercial vehicles[1] (thousands)	Passenger cars[2] (thousands)	Passenger cars per thousand population	Percentage increase in passenger cars 1964–1975
United Kingdom	2,000	14,080	251	68
Belgium	319	2,535	259	120
Denmark	221	1,256	248	86
France	2,210	15,180	288	72
Germany (FR)	1,349	17,356	280	117
Irish Republic	60	508	164	97
Italy	1,141	14,295	257	206
Luxembourg	13	128	357	129
Netherlands	362	3,500	257	231
Japan	10,928	15,854	143	848
USA	25,464	105,287	495	47

1. Excluding trailers and farm tractors.
2. Vehicles seating not more than nine persons, including taxis, jeeps and station wagons.

Table 196

**Road accidents
1975**

	Persons killed (Death occuring within thirty days of accident)	Persons injured	Rate per 100 million vehicle/kms	
			Persons killed	Persons injured
Great Britain	6,366	318,584	2·6	132
Belgium	2,329	82,147	7·0	245
Denmark	827	20,100	4·0[1]	92[1]
France	13,170[2]	353,730	5·7	152
Germany (FR)	14,870	457,797	5·0	154
Irish Republic	586	7,198	..	..
Italy	9,511[3]	229,898	5·9[1]	143[1]
Luxembourg	122	2,628	..	..
Netherlands	2,321	59,979	3·9[4]	101[4]
Japan	10,792[5]	622,467	3·0	175
USA[4]	46,049[6]	2,653,000	2·2	128

1. 1972.
2. Deaths occuring within 6 days.
3. Deaths occuring within 7 days.
4. 1974.
5. Deaths occurring within 24 hours.
6. Deaths occurring within 1 year.

Table 197

Televisions and telephones
1975

	Television receivers in use		Telephones in use	
	Thousands	Per 1,000 population	Thousands	Per 1,000 population
United Kingdom	17,641	315	20,536	366
Belgium	2,464	252	2,667	272
Denmark	1,556	308	2,164	428
France	12,335	235	12,405	236
Germany (FR)	18,920	305	18,767	302
Irish Republic	550	178	394	127
Italy	11,817	213	13,695	246
Luxembourg	88	257	142	397
Netherlands	3,510	259	4,679	344
Japan	25,564	233	39,405	356
USA	121,100	571	143,972	677
USSR	52,500	208	15,782	62

Table 198
Education
1976

	Age limits		Duration of compulsory education (years)
	Pre-school	Compulsory education	
United Kingdom	2–5	5–16	11
Belgium	3–6	6–14	8
Denmark	5–7	7–16	9
France	2–5	6–16	10
Germany (FR)	3–7	6–18[1]	12[1]
Irish Republic	4–5	6–15	9
Italy	3–6	6–13	8
Luxembourg	4–6	6–15	9
Netherlands	4–6	6–16	10
Japan	3–5	6–15	9
USA	3–6	7–16	10
USSR	3–7	7–15/16	8–9

1. Including 3 years of compulsory part-time vocational education.

Table 199
Economically active population

	Year	Total population Thousands	Economically active population Thousands	Percentage	Female percentage of total economically active
United Kingdom	1973	55,933	25,287	45·2	36·3
Belgium	1975	9,813	4,003	40·8	34·4
Denmark	1974	5,054	2,479	49·0	40·9
France	1976	52,842	20,641	41·6	36·1
Germany (FR)	1975	61,886	26,878	43·4	37·2
Irish Republic	1974	3.086	1,122	36·4	25·7[1]
Italy	1976	55,274	19,615	35·5	28·3
Luxembourg	1975	359	150	42·0	26·2[2]
Netherlands	1971	13,060	4,789	36·7	25·9
Japan	1975	111,934	54,375	48·6	36·8
USA	1970	213,137	94,793	44·5	39·1
USSR	1970	241,720	117,028	48·4	50·4

1. 1971.
2. 1970.

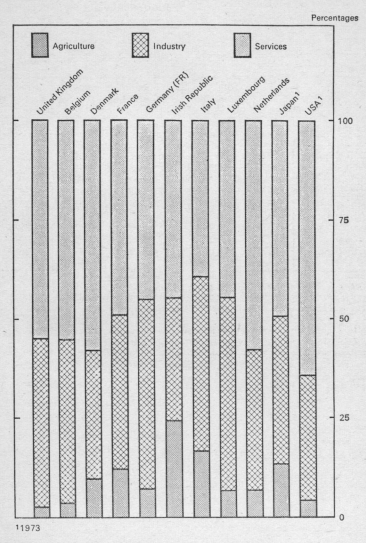

**Chart 39: Civilian employment
by sector
1974**

11973

Table 200
Unemployment

annual averages

	Code	1971		1976	
		Thousands	Percentage	Thousands	Percentage
United Kingdom	a	799·1	3·5	1,331·8	5·7
Belgium[1]	a	70·9	2·9	215·1	8·1
Denmark	b	30·0	3·7	82·6	7·6
France	a	338·2	..	813·0[2]	..
Germany (FR)	a	185·1	0·8	921·0	4·0
Irish Republic[3]	c	42·4	7·2	81·0	12·0
Italy	d	609·0	3·2	693·0	3·5
Luxembourg	a	0·02	..	0·33	..
Netherlands	a	62·0	1·6	194·1	4·7
Japan	d	640·0	1·2	1,040·0	1·9
USA	d	4,993·0	5·9	7,655·0	8·0

Codes *a Registered unemployed: employment office statistics.*
b Statistics of trade unions and union benefit fund statistics.
c Compulsory unemployment insurance statistics.
d Labour force surveys.

1. Unemployed receiving insurance benefits.
2. Excluding some unemployed over 60 years of age.
3. Excluding agriculture, fishing and private domestic services.

Table 201
Index of industrial production
1970 = 100

	1969	1971	1972	1973	1974	1975
United Kingdom	100	100	103	110	106	101
Belgium	97	103	109	116	120	108
Denmark[1]	97	102	110	115	109	103
France	94	106	113	121	125	114
Germany (FR)	94	102	106	113	111	105
Irish Republic	96	104	109	121	125	117
Italy	94	100	104	114	120	108
Luxembourg	100	99	103	114	119	93
Netherlands	92	106	111	118	121	115
Japan	88	103	110	127	124	110
USA	103	102	111	120	120	109
USSR	93	108	115	123	133	143

1. Manufacturing industry only.

Table 202
Index of consumer prices
1970 = 100

	1971	1972	1973	1974	1975	1976
United Kingdom	109	117	128	149	185	215
Belgium	104	110	118	133	150	163
Denmark	106	113	123	142	156	170
France	105	112	120	136	152	168
Germany (FR)	105	111	119	127	135	141
Irish Republic	109	118	132	154	186	220
Italy	105	111	123	146	171	200
Luxembourg	104	110	117	128	142	156
Netherlands	108	116	126	138	152	165
Japan	106	111	124	154	172	188
USA	104	108	114	127	139	146
USSR	100	100	100	100	100	..

Table 203

Gross domestic product at current market prices

Eur[1] thousand million

	1965	1970	1972	1973	1974	1975
United Kingdom	99·3	121·7	143·6	140·4	152·8	172·5
Belgium	16·6	25·2	31·6	35·9	42·0	46·2
Denmark	10·1	15·6	19·2	21·8	24·3	26·9
France	96·8	140·9	176·6	200·5	212·6	253·3
Germany (FR)	114·3	185·5	235·7	275·4	305·8	319·9
Irish Republic	2·7	3·9	5·1	5·2	5·4	5·9
Italy	58·4	92·7	109·4	112·7	122·1	130·2
Luxembourg	0·7	1·1	1·2	1·5	1·7	1·7
Netherlands	18·7	31·6	41·7	48·4	55·8	61·2
Japan	89·0	196·9	270·9	327·5	365·6	372·8
USA	690·0	984·4	1,076·0	1,041·2	1,125·8	1,149·7

Table 204

Exchange rates used in above table

Counterpart of 1 Eur[1] in national currency

	Currency	1965	1970	1972	1973	1974	1975
United Kingdom	Pound Sterling	0·357	0·417	0·437	0·511	0·534	0·597
Belgium	Francs	50·000	50·000	48·657	48·657	48·657	48·657
Denmark	Kroner	6·907	7·500	7·578	7·578	7·578	7·578
France	Francs	4·937	5·554	5·554	5·554	6·010	5·680
Germany (FR)	Deutsche Marks	4·000	3·660	3·499	3·328	3·220	3·220
Irish Republic	£ sterling	0·357	0·417	0·437	0·511	0·534	0·597
Italy	Lire	625·000	625·000	631·342	729·000	813·000	863·000
Luxembourg	Francs	50·000	50·000	48·657	48·657	48·657	48·657
Netherlands	Guilders	3·620	3·620	3·523	3·474	3·355	3·355
Japan	Yen	360·000	360·000	334·400	339·000	363·000	389·000
USA	Dollars	1·000	1·000	1·086	1·250	1·250	1·320

1. Eur – the unit of account of the European Communities; the national currency counterparts are calculated on the basis of official parities declared to the IMF, or market rates in the case of floating currencies.

EEC statistics

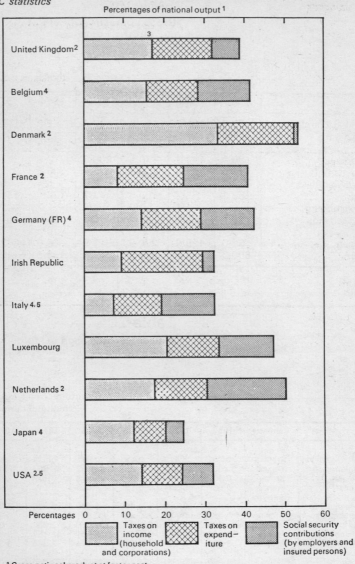

Percentages of national output [1]

Chart 40: Taxation and social security contributions as percentage of national output, 1974

[1] Gross national product at factor cost
[2] Based on the new international system of national accounts
[3] After deducting tax credits
[4] Based on the former international system of national accounts
[5] 1973 data

Table 205
**Average annual rates of growth
1965–75**

At constant prices

percentage

	Gross domestic product at market prices		Gross domestic product at market prices per person employed
	Total	Per capita	
United Kingdom	2·2	1·9	2·3
Belgium	4·2	3·8	3·8
Denmark	3·2	2·6	2·7
France	4·7	3·8	4·0
Germany (FR)	3·2	2·6	3·8
Irish Republic[1]	2·4	1·5	2·9
Italy	4·1	3 3	4·0
Luxembourg	2·9	1·8	1·3
Netherlands	4·4	3·3	4·1
Japan	8·2	6·9	7·3
USA	2·6	1·6	0·9

1. 1970–75.

Table 206

Consumption of energy per head of population
1975

Country of arrival	Energy[1] Total Tce[2]	Electricity Industrial uses Kwh[3]	Electricity Other uses Kwh[3]
United Kingdom	5·470	1,673	2,487
Belgium	6·614	2,208	1,426
Denmark	5·076	909	2,352
France	4·763	1,677	1,514
Germany (FR)	6·001	2,273	2,172
Irish Republic	3·326	755	1,243
Italy	3·394	1,411	887
Luxembourg	22·132	6,574	2,089
Netherlands	6·354	1,776	1,812
Japan[3]	4·014	2,082	1,780
USA[3]	11·907	3,525	4,990
USSR[3]	5·359	2,300	1,160

1. 1974.
2. Ton coal equivalent.
3. Kilowatt hour.

Table 207

External trade[1]
1974

	Exports (f.o.b.[2])			Imports (c.i.f.[3])		
	Eur million	% of GNP	Eur per head	Eur million	% of GNP	Eur per head
United Kingdom	30,906	20·4	551	43,292	28·6	772
Denmark	6,191	25·3	1,227	7,936	32·5	1,573
France	36,072	16·9	687	41,717	19·6	795
Germany (FR)	71,589	23·5	1,154	55,589	18·2	896
Irish Republic	2,106	39·6	682	3,049	57·3	988
Italy	24,209	20·3	437	32,529	27·1	587
Belgium ⎫ Luxembourg⎭	22,550	51·5	2,226	23,723	54·2	2,342
Netherlands	26,386	47·6	1,948	26,576	47·9	1,962
Japan	44,478	12·2	406	49,628	13·6	453
USA[4]	77,714	6·9	367	80,778	7·2	381
USSR	21,924	..	87	19,911	..	79

1. General trade for the United Kingdom and Denmark; special trade in all other cases.
2. Free on board.
3. Cost, insurance and freight.
4. Imports f.o.b.

Table 208

Balance of trade[1]

Eur million

	1970	1971	1972	1973	1974	1975
United Kingdom	−2,372	−1,111	−3,227	−6,652	−12,386	−7,145
Denmark	−1,095	− 969	− 662	−1,210	−1,745	−1,245
France	−1,184	− 713	− 790	−1,122	−5,645	−1,571
Germany (FR)	+4,375	+4,699	+5,937	+10,132	+16,000	+11,577
Irish Republic	− 534	− 528	− 449	− 527	− 943	− 435
Italy	−1,763	− 856	− 657	−4,465	−8,320	−2,735
Belgium ⎫ Luxembourg⎭	+ 247	− 366	+ 601	+ 361	−1,173	−1,442
Netherlands	−1,626	−1,151	− 431	− 284	− 190	+130
Japan	+ 437	+4,308	+4,720	+1,108	−5,150	−1,543
USA	+3,263	−1,465	−5,416	+1,757	−3,065	+7,624
USSR	+1,061	+1,327	− 632	+ 280	+2,013	−2,770

1. + denotes an export surplus; − denotes an import surplus.

Units of measurement

Conversion from metric

	Equivalent values
Length	
1 millimetre (mm)	0·039 inches
1 centimetre (cm) = 10 millimetres	0·394 inches
1 metre (m) = 100 centimetres	1·094 yards
1 kilometre (km) = 1,000 metres	0·621 miles
Area	
1 square centimetre (sq. cm)	0·155 square inches
1 square metre (sq. m) = 10,000 square centimetres	1·196 square yards
1 hectare (ha) = 10,000 square metres	2·471 acres
1 square kilometre (sq. km) = million square metres	0·386 square miles
Volume	
1 cubic centimetre (cc)	0·061 cubic inches
1 cubic metre (cu. m) = million cubic centimetres	1·308 cubic yards
Capacity	
1 litre (l)	1·760 pints
1 hectolitre (hl) = 100 litres	22·000 gallons
Weight	
1 gramme (g)	0·035 ounces
1 hectogramme (hg) = 100 grammes	3·528 ounces
1 kilogramme (kg) = 10 hectogrammes	2·205 pounds
1 tonne (t) = 1,000 kilogrammes	0·984 long tons = 1·102 short tons

Units of measurement

Conversion to metric

	Equivalent values
Length	
1 inch (in.)	25·400 millimetres or 2·540 centimetres
1 foot (ft) = 12 inches	0·305 metres
1 yard (yd) = 3 feet	0·914 metres
1 mile = 1,760 yards	1·609 kilometres
Area	
1 square inch (sq. in.)	6·452 square centimetres
1 square foot (sq. ft) = 144 square inches	929·030 square centimetres
1 square yard (sq. yd) = 9 square feet	0·836 square metres
1 acre = 4,840 square yards	0·405 hectares
1 square mile (sq. mile) = 640 acres	259·000 hectares or 2·590 square kilometres
Volume	
1 cubic foot (cu. ft)	0·028 cubic metres
1 cubic yard (cu. yd) = 27 cubic feet	0·765 cubic metres
Capacity	
1 pint	0·568 litres
1 gallon = 8 pints	4·546 litres
Weight	
1 ounce avoirdupois (oz.) = 16 ounces	28·350 grammes
1 pound avoirdupois (lb.) = 112 pounds	453·592 grammes or 0·454 kilogrammes
1 hundredweight (cwt)	50·800 kilogrammes
1 short ton = 2,000 pounds	0·907 tonnes
1 long ton = 2,240 pounds	1·016 tonnes

Index of sources

The following pages offer some guidance to the sources of material included in *Facts in Focus*. In general, these sources contain the figures in much greater detail and give other related information, e.g. explanatory notes and definitions.

Most of the data used originate in Government Statistics Departments, but other organizations outside Government have also supplied material.

Apart from the original sources, the following general statistical publications are useful in providing supplementary information: *Annual Abstract of Statistics, Regional Statistics* and the *Monthly Digest of Statistics* with its annual Supplement of *Definitions and Explanatory Notes*. United Kingdom figures in the EEC section have been brought up to date wherever possible.

Tables and charts	Government department or other organization supplying data	Publications
I Population and vital statistics		
1–2, 6–10, *Charts 1–3*	Office of Population Censuses and Surveys	Registrar General's Statistical Review
		OPCS Monitors PP and FM
	General Register Office, Scotland	Annual Report of the Registrar General for Scotland
	General Register Office, Northern Ireland	Annual Report of the Registrar General for Northern Ireland
		Quarterly returns for England and Wales, Scotland and Northern Ireland
		Population Trends
1	Government Actuary's Department	OPCS Monitor PP2
3	Office of Population Censuses and Surveys	OPCS Monitor PP1 77/1
4	Office of Population Censuses and Surveys	Annual Estimates of Population for England and Wales and of Local Authority areas
		OPCS Monitor PP1 No. 2
	General Register Office, Scotland	Annual Estimates of Population of Scotland
5	Office of Population Censuses and Surveys	Sample Census 1966 Household Composition Tables
		Census 1971 Great Britain Summary Tables
II Health		
13	Central Statistical Office	Annual Abstract of Statistics
14–15, 17, 19, 22, 23, *Chart 4*	Department of Health and Social Security	Digest of Health Statistics for England and Wales
	Department of Health and Social Security	Social Security Statistics 1973

Tables and charts	Government department or other organization supplying data	Publications
16, 18	Office of Population Censuses and Surveys	Registrar General's Statistical Review for England and Wales, Part I
		OPCS Monitors DH2 and MB2
	General Register Office, Scotland	Annual Report of the Registrar General for Scotland
	General Register Office, Northern Ireland	Annual Report of the Registrar General for Northern Ireland
20	Office of Population Censuses and Surveys	Registrar General's Statistical Review for England and Wales, Supplement on Abortion
		OPCS Monitor AB
	Scottish Home and Health Department	Health Bulletin
21	Family Planning Association	Annual Report and Accounts
24	Home Office	Unpublished

III Social Security

25	Central Statistical Office	Annual Abstract of Statistics
26–31, Chart 5	Department of Health and Social Security	Social Security Statistics

IV Justice and Law

32	Home Office	Report of HM Chief Inspector of Constabulary, England and Wales
	Scottish Home and Health Department	Report of HM Chief Inspector of Constabulary, Scotland
	Ministry of Home Affairs (Northern Ireland)	Report on the Administration of Home Office Services, Northern Ireland
33–36, 38, 40	Home Office	Criminal Statistics, England and Wales
	Scottish Home and Health Department	Criminal Statistics, Scotland
	Ministry of Home Affairs (Northern Ireland)	Report on the Administration of Home Office Services, Northern Ireland
37	Home Office	Unpublished
39	Lord Chancellor's Office Scottish Home and Health Department	Annual Report on Legal Aid and Advice
41–43, Chart 6	Home Office	Report on the Work of the Prison Department
		Criminal Statistics, England and Wales
44	Home Office	Return of Election Expenses
		Vachers Parliamentary Companion

Tables and charts	Government department or other organization supplying data	Publications
V Housing		
45–51, *Chart 7*	Department of the Environment	Housing and Construction Statistics
51	Department of the Environment	House condition survey: England and Wales, 1967 (Economic Trends, May 1968) House condition survey: England and Wales, 1971 (Housing Survey Reports No. 9)
52	Department of the Environment	Unpublished
VI Transport and communications		
53, 56–59	Department of Transport	Transport Statistics (GB)
	Scottish Development Department	Transport Statistics (GB)
	Welsh Office	Business Monitor
54, 61, 62, *Chart 8*	Department of Transport British Railways Board London Transport Executive	Transport Statistics (GB)
55	Greater London Council	Annual Abstract of Greater London Statistics
Chart 9	Department of Transport	Road Accidents in Great Britain
60	Scottish Development Department	
Chart 10	Department of Employment	Family Expenditure Survey
63–64	Civil Aviation Authority	Civil Aviation Authority monthly statistics
65	Department of Trade and Industry	Trade and Industry
66	Civil Aviation Authority	Accidents to Aircraft on the British Register
67	Department of Industry	Registry of Ships, published by Registrar General of Shipping and Seamen
68	Department of Industry	Overseas Trade Accounts of the United Kingdom
69	National Ports Council	Annual Digest of Ports Statistics
70	Post Office	Post Office Report and Accounts
VII Environment		
71–73, *Charts 11–12*	Meteorological Office	Monthly Weather Report
74	Office of Population Censuses and Surveys	Central Statistical Office: Annual Abstract of Statistics
75	Department of the Environment	
76	Forestry Commission	Annual Report of the Forestry Commissioners
	Ministry of Agriculture (Northern Ireland)	Northern Ireland Digest of Statistics

Tables and charts	Government department or other organization supplying data	Publications
77	Department of the Environment Department of Trade and Industry Scottish Development Department	National Survey of Air Pollution 1961–1971, Vol. 1
78, Chart 13	Department of the Environment Welsh Office Scottish Development Department London Weather Centre	Report of a River Pollution Survey of England and Wales Towards Cleaner Water – Report of a River Pollution Survey of Scotland Memorandum No. 5 Appendix A

VIII Education

79	Central Statistical Office	Annual Abstract of Statistics
80–94, Charts 14–15	Department of Education and Science University Grants Committee	Statistics of Education: England and Wales Vol. 1 Schools Vol. 2 School leavers, GCE and CSE Vol. 3 Further Education Vol. 4 Teachers Vol. 5 Finance and Awards Vol. 6 Universities (United Kingdom)
80, 92	Scottish Education Department Department and Ministry of Education, Northern Ireland	Scottish Educational Statistics Northern Ireland Education Statistics
95	University Grants Committee	First Destination of University Graduates
96–98	Central Statistical Office	Studies in Official Statistics, No. 27: Research and Development Expenditure and Employment

IX Manpower and earnings

99	Office of Population Censuses and Surveys	Census 1951, Great Britain Economic Activity tables Census 1961, Great Britain Economic Activity tables Census 1971, Great Britain Economic Activity tables
100, 102, 104–112, Charts 16–19	Department of Employment	Department of Employment Gazette
101	Government Actuary's Department	Unpublished
103	Civil Service Department	Civil Service Statistics
108–109	Department of Employment	Central Statistical Office: Monthly Digest of Statistics New Earnings Survey

Tables and charts	Government department or other organization supplying data	Publications
X Leisure		
Chart 20	Department of Employment	Department of Employment Gazette
113–114	Office of Population Censuses and Surveys	General Household Survey
115	Department of Industry	Trade and Industry
	Post Office	Post Office Report and Accounts
Chart 21	Football League	Unpublished
	Department of Industry	Trade and Industry
	Post Office	Post Office Report and Accounts
116	British Broadcasting Corporation	Unpublished
117, *Chart 22*	Department of Industry	Business Monitor (Overseas Travel and Tourism)
	British Tourist Authority	British National Travel Survey
118	British Tourist Authority	Home Tourism Survey
XI Agriculture, fisheries and food		
119–123, 125, *Charts 24–25*	Ministry of Agriculture, Fisheries and Food	Agricultural Statistics Output and Utilisation of Farm Produce in the United Kingdom
Chart 23	Ministry of Agriculture, Fisheries and Food	A Century of Agricultural Statistics
124	Ministry of Agriculture, Fisheries and Food	Central Statistical Office: Economic Trends, November 1971
126	Ministry of Agriculture, Fisheries and Food	Sea Fisheries Statistical Tables
	Department of Agriculture and Fisheries for Scotland	Scottish Sea Fisheries Statistical Tables
XII Production		
Chart 26	Central Statistical Office	National Income and Expenditure Economic Trends
127, 130–134, *Chart 27*	Department of Industry	Trade and Industry Business Monitor
128	British Steel Corporation and British Independent Steel Producers' Association	Annual Statistics for the United Kingdom
129	World Bureau of Metal Statistics	World Metal Statistics
135	HM Customs and Excise	Annual Report of the Commissioners of HM Customs and Excise
136	Department of the Environment	Housing and Construction Statistics

Tables and charts	Government department or other organization supplying data	Publications
136	Department of Industry	Business Monitor
137	Department of Industry Department of the Environment	Trade and Industry

XIII Energy

138–145, Charts 28–29	Department of Energy	Digest of United Kingdom Energy Statistics

XIV Distributive and service trades

146–148	Department of Industry Business Statistics Office	Census of Distribution and Other Services Business Monitor SD Series
149, 151	Department of Industry	Board of Trade Journal (now Trade and Industry)
150	Department of Industry	Trade and Industry Catering Trades 1969, statistical inquiry

XV National income and expenditure

152–161, Charts 30–32	Central Statistical Office	National Income and Expenditure Economic Trends

XVI Personal income and expenditure

162, 171, Chart 34	Central Statistical Office	National Income and Expenditure
163	Central Statistical Office	Economic Trends Monthly Digest of Statistics
164–167, 174	Board of Inland Revenue	Inland Revenue Statistics
168	Central Statistical Office	Economic Trends, 1964, 1969, December 1974, 1975 and 1976
169	Central Statistical Office	Available on request
170	Department of Employment	Department of Employment Gazette
172–173, Chart 33	Department of Employment	Family Expenditure Survey

XVII Financial statistics

175–176	Central Statistical Office Bank of England	Central Statistical Office: Financial Statistics
177	Bank of England	Quarterly Bulletin Central Statistical Office: Financial Statistics
178	Building Societies Association Central Statistical Office	Financial Statistics
179	Department of Trade	Insurance Business Statistics
180	Central Statistical Office	Financial Statistics

Tables and charts	Government department or other organization supplying data	Publications
181	Department of National Savings	Annual Report of the National Savings Committee
		Annual Report of the Inspection Committee of the Trustee Savings Banks
		Accounts of the National Savings Banks
182	Bank of England	Central Statistical Office: Financial Statistics
183, *Chart 35*	Bank of England, Financial Times, Institute of Actuaries and Faculty of Actuaries	Central Statistical Office: Financial Statistics

XVIII External transactions

184, 188, *Chart 36*	Central Statistical Office	United Kingdom Balance of Payments
		Economic Trends
		Financial Statistics
185–187, *Chart 37*	Department of Trade	Central Statistical Office: United Kingdom Balance of Payments

XIX EEC statistics

189	UN	Demographic Yearbook
191–192		Monthly Bulletin of Statistics
Chart 38 190, 205–208	SOEC	Basic Statistics of the Community
193	World Health Organization	World Health Statistics, Vol. III
194–195	UN	Statistical Yearbook
196	International Road Federation	World Road Statistics
197	UNESCO	Statistical Yearbook
	UN	Statistical Yearbook
198	UNESCO	Statistical Yearbook
199	ILO	Yearbook of Labour Statistics
200, 202	ILO	Yearbook of Labour Statistics
		Bulletin of Labour Statistics
Chart 39	OECD	Labour Force Statistics
	ILO	Yearbook of Labour Statistics
201	UN	Statistical Yearbook
		Monthly Bulletin of Statistics
203–204	EEC	National Accounts
Chart 40	OECD	National Accounts of OECD countries